Hamlyn all-

Francis

Archaeology

illustrated by Angus McBride

Hamlyn - London
Sun Books - Melbourne

FOREWORD

Archaeology is a complex subject that does not sit well in the text-book mould. Working archaeologists have to grapple daily with concepts that do not go easily into the traditional work of popularization. In this publication an attempt is made to induce familiarity by repeating themes and terms so that some of the vocabulary of archaeology can be painlessly mastered.

This publication tries to give a broad selection of themes which will enable even a beginner to look at museum displays with understanding or to consult periodicals like *Antiquity*.

Every page of this book became potentially out of date the moment it was printed. The pace of archaeological research is now very fast and most datings, especially radiocarbon ones, are being drastically re-assessed.

F.C.

Published by The Hamlyn Publishing Group Ltd
London · New York · Sydney · Toronto
Hamlyn House, Feltham, Middlesex, England
In association with Sun Books Pty. Ltd. Melbourne.

ISBN 0 600 00114 8
Photoset by BAS Printers Limited, Wallop, Hampshire
Colour separations by Schwitter Limited, Zurich
Printed by Smeets, Weert, Holland

CONTENTS

Left: L. S. B. Leakey Right: Sir Mortimer Wheeler

INTRODUCTION

To many the word archaeology conjures up images of great ruined temples and cities: Mohenjo Daro, Macchu Picchu, Zimbabwe, Angkor Vat, the great structures of the Nile Valley and many others. Such remains easily excite the imagination and the layman is tempted to believe that archaeology deals mainly with monuments of this kind. But this book puts little emphasis on the archaeology of the obviously impressive; instead it tries to show the story of man through his everyday objects. Rather than describe large-scale excavations, these pages will show far more of the way the archaeologist grapples with the facts he discovers. It is better when learning the elements of archaeology to face the incompleteness of man's story and to see how provisional are many archaeological world-pictures.

Space will not permit a description of many cultures and sites so there is no mention of the Khazars or the Picts or the Olmecs. All the same the reader will be given a selection

Left: A. Pitt Rivers Centre: H. Schliemann Right: H. Breuil

that will give him a sense of general patterns and developments. It will be possible to see what preceded what and to grasp the strange back-and-forth fluctuations in the complex story of man in the past.

A word should be said about archaeologists. Many work unobtrusively but they are of the same breed as the early pioneers and thinkers of archaeology. Famous archaeologists like H. Schliemann, General A. Pitt Rivers and Alfred Rust made a vigorous entry into the subject rather late in their careers. Others like the Dane, C. J. Thomsen, or the Australian, V. G. Childe were gentle persons who had powerful pioneering minds ideal for new interpretations. Some mingled energy in the field with profundity in the study or library: the French priest Henri Breuil, Pei-Wen-Chung from China or the Briton, L. S. B. Leakey. Today the archaeologist has to be scholar, teacher, organizer, and, above all, a leader. Sir Mortimer Wheeler, R. Braidwood and R. Heizer are precursors of this type of archaeologist.

This book is for the newcomer to the subject. It is not for the kind of newcomer who thinks that archaeology is only about golden treasures, or lost cities or buried Pharaohs. Archaeologists often spend most of their time dealing with what is left of the day-to-day belongings of very ordinary people. Such remains are not found by expeditions to glamorous sites in Egypt or Cambodia, but almost accidentally such as when an underground railway is constructed in Milan or when a motorway in Mexico near Popocatepetl or an atomic power station in north Britain is being built.

Archaeology studies the story of man's past through his

Many important finds have been made by chance during building operations. Prompt contact with a museum is necessary to prevent knowledge being lost.

material remains and traces. We say 'traces' because footprints of Stone Age man have been found in the soft earth of some ancient caves. Archaeology is both an art and a science which can bring its special techniques to bear on any period. The earliest stone tools made by man are obvious material for the archaeologist's skills, but so is a nineteenth-century water-mill or canal lock. There is no rigid time limit for archaeology. The only criterion is: will the archaeologist be the best person to sort out the story of this site or period?

The archaeology of no country can be studied in isolation. For example, an archaeologist working in Ecuador excavates a coastal site of about 3200 B.C., and finds fragments of pottery with grooved patterns. Though he records these faithfully, he would not be doing his job if he did not look elsewhere for parallels. That the best parallels are found in Japan's Island of Kyushu over 8000 miles (13,000 km.) away is exciting and provocative. The Japanese pottery from that island is similar but one must not start theorizing too quickly about voyages from Japan to Ecuador. Were there intermediate stages? Or are the similarities just coincidences. By a continuous dialogue the archaeologist, whether professional or amateur, tries to get at a truth eroded by time.

Archaeology, so much a subject for experts, also needs great discipline. It is this quality that enables the amateur to contribute – not so much by digging as by skilled observation and speedy reporting of finds. This book tries to educate the beginner and make him more perceptive.

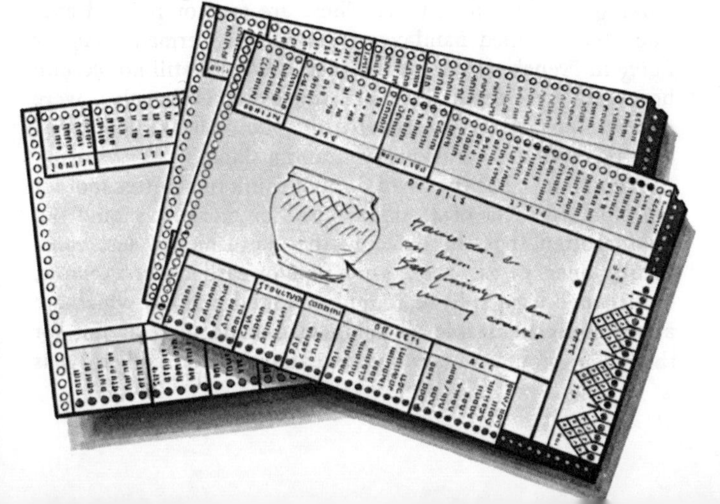

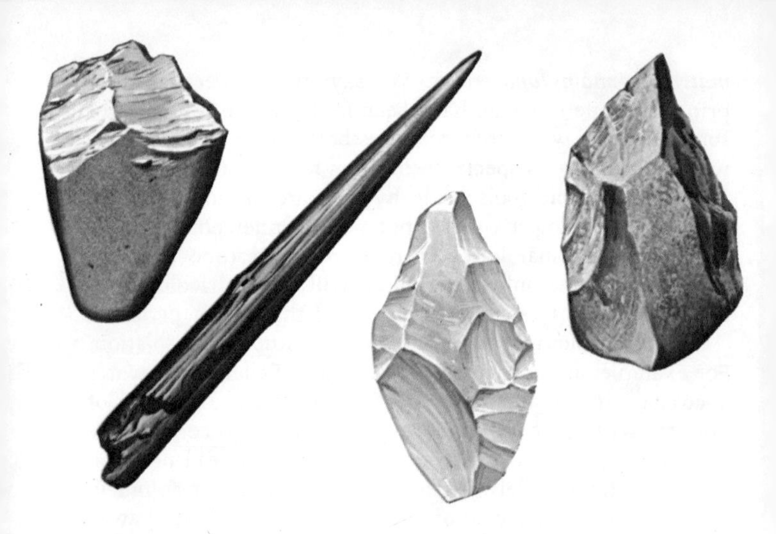

Pebble tool ; yew spear head ; handaxes from India and Africa

PREHISTORY OF THE OLD AND NEW WORLDS

Old Stone Age or Palaeolithic

In Europe, Africa and Asia there have been found stone tools in flint and other available stone which are relics of people who lived literally hundreds of thousands of years ago. In gravels, and river deposits and even on the ground surface in Africa, observers have picked the more obvious looking of these stone tools. These are oval or pointed axe-like objects called handaxes (*Faustkeil* in German, *Coup de Poing* in French, *Amigdale* in Italian). We are still not certain how they were used. The usual suggestion is that they were general purpose tools used for grubbing, hacking, prising and, possibly, for occasionally cleaning skins.

Though it seems that man did not think of a better tool for perhaps a quarter of a million years or more, it should not be forgotten that there were other implements, less spectacular ones, in use at the same time or earlier. For example, earlier men used split or roughly pointed pebbles which are almost unrecognizable as being man-made were it not for their being found in certain contexts in some numbers. It is important to note that iron wheels produce good flakes.

Besides the chunky handaxe there were less shapely chopping tools and choppers. But here one should emphasize that man also used *flakes* of stone adroitly and, sometimes, maladroitly, struck. Some early items need an experienced eye to recognize, but later developments show that a large piece of stone was carefully prepared so that one tap with something heavy could produce a sharp flake with strong cutting or scraping edges arranged as the tool maker wanted.

Occasionally evidence of wooden spear heads has been found and in Africa and elsewhere there are finds that have led archaeologists to suggest that wood and antler tools were used. Most of the non-stone tools of early man have perished as have the majority of his physical remains.

In China and Africa sites have been found where fire was used: so cooking was not unknown to Palaeolithic man. We cannot know much about the culture of these hunter-gatherers. Paradoxically we know more about the extremes of cold they survived in the Ice Age and of the warm conditions that punctuated retreats of the ice. Some of the animals they saw were similar to those of today but many, such as the mammoth, have long been extinct.

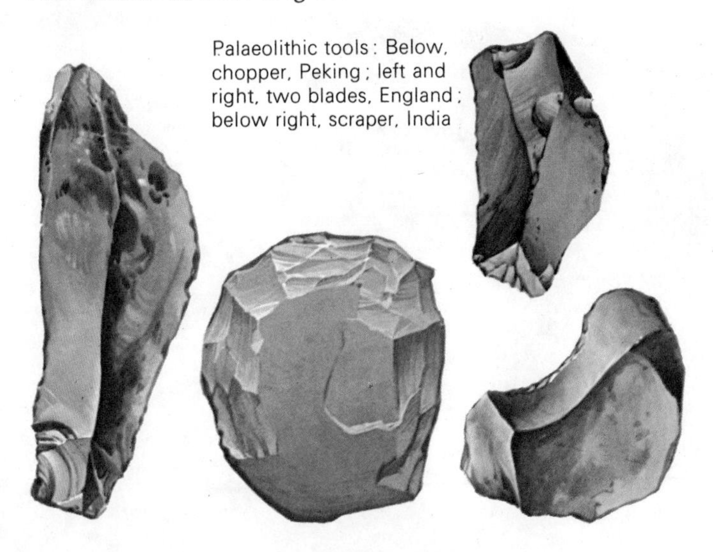

Palaeolithic tools: Below, chopper, Peking; left and right, two blades, England; below right, scraper, India

Stone Age man's environment

Most people have heard of the 'Ice Age' but they have no idea of its date, duration or extent. Starting with events near our own time, we can say that around 12,000 B.C. the ice sheets in the northern hemisphere were on the retreat. The ice had not covered the world and there were times when parts of Siberia were not glaciated. The ice advanced and retreated several times, and there were between glaciations, periods of considerable warmth known as interglacials.

How do we measure and identify this period during which man as we know him came on the scene? The period is named the Pleistocene, and geologists prefer to recognize it by its distinctive animal fossils which range from mammoths to small rodents. The geologist can also map the time sequence by looking for evidence of cold and warm periods.

Each decade of research has increased the length of the Pleistocene period. Earlier estimates of around 600,000 years are now quadrupled, but man's status and environment at the start of the Pleistocene is still problematic.

Ice age deposits I interglacial : II glacial. Symbols show tool finds

Evidence of frost cracks

Fortunately gravels or the wind-blown loess deposits of the Pleistocene are not the only keys to chronology. Deep borings in the Atlantic and the Pacific have produced detailed evidence of past climatic history.

Perhaps the most difficult aspect in the dating of Pleistocene deposits containing man or his tools is that encountered in areas far from the two poles: areas such as the Sahara Desert. There one cannot find deposits reflecting glacial or periglacial conditions. Accordingly, geologists have postulated the existence of rainy or pluvial periods to correspond with glacial periods. Evidence of 'Pluvials' and 'Interpluvials' has helped date some human deposits, but the investigations can be fraught with errors.

The glacial and interglacial periods, as is to be expected, affected the levels of the oceans and seas as well as rivers and lakes connected with them. Very often an 'ancient shoreline' well inland has furnished a clue to Palaeolithic settlement. It should not be forgotten that in parts of the world some previously-occupied areas are under water.

Lower Palaeolithic in Europe, Asia and Africa

While it is possible to suggest that there were no great cultural changes in the half-million or more years before the Ice Age ended, there were in the Palaeolithic many varieties of tools which have been named from the places where they were first recorded. The beginner is asked to bear with such technical terms as a first step in his growing familiarization with archaeological objects.

The earliest *pebble-tools* to merit systematic study have been named *Oldowan* from the African finding place. Later came man's first standardized tool the *hand-axe,* the earlier rougher ones called *Abbevillian* and the later, more elegant ones *Acheulian.* Man probably used flakes quite early, but among the first to be noted in local concentrations are, to give examples, the thick *Clactonian* flakes and the early *Punjabi* flakes. Later man became more skilful in removing from stone cores thin flakes of planned pattern. The technique, usually named after finds of the *Levallois* culture in France, was an impressive one.

Though hand-axes were made in a vast arc from Southern

Areas where handaxes are found

Area of cultures without handaxes

Africa to India, the Far East tended to make its own variants of Palaeolithic tools. In China at Chou K'ou Tien, rough 'choppers' and 'chopping-tools' and flakes were made by 'Peking Man' rather than handaxes of the Acheulian type. In the Indian sub-continent one finds examples of the *Soan* choppers (cores flaked or sharpened on one side of an edge) and chopping tools (cores which were flaked on both sides of the cutting edge).

Central and Southern Africa developed local variants of the Palaeolithic cultures. The *Sangoan,* which is nearer the times of the last glaciation in Europe, and definitely after the African Acheulian, was a jungle culture with *'picks', lance-heads* and a broad-edged *axe.* Another post-Acheulian culture was the *Fauresmith* which had flakes as well as core tools and has been found from Kenya to South Africa.

Each excavation season produces more far-flung examples of early Palaeolithic cultures. Crude Palaeolithic tools have turned up in Japan and doubtless others will be found in other parts of the world. Hardly to be classified in the Lower Palaeolithic are some tools of Palaeolithic type found in Australia. These go back to almost 20,000 B.C.

Homo sapiens neanderthalensis or Mousterian man

Neanderthal Man

Earlier books on archaeology have often shown Neanderthal Man as a brutal-faced, shambling creature. This is a misleading picture of the kind of man who is thought to have disappeared between forty and thirty thousand years ago. One cannot say whether he was killed off or pushed into inhospitable areas, or whether he 'merged' into modern man.

Though best known from French and European excavations, his bones and distinctive stone tools have also been found in North Africa, and in the Near and Middle East. He

Early flint implements

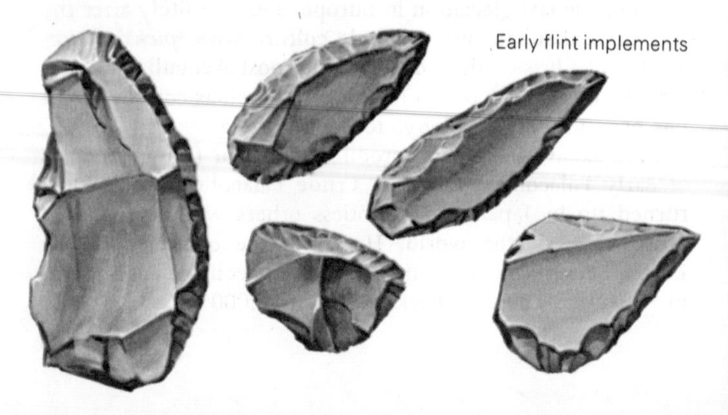

lived largely in the cold world of the last glaciation, but the conditions were often far from arctic.

He was a skilled maker of tools in flint. He made hand-axes not unlike those of the earlier Acheulian culture; he knew the Levallois technique of striking sharp, shaped flakes from a carefully prepared core of flint. His later tool kit contained some flint 'blades' which are distinctive of the Upper or Advanced Palaeolithic of men looking like ourselves who dominated the scene by the end of the ice age.

Neanderthal Man types probably go back many thousands of years, so that it becomes clear that we have information on only the last phases. Often Neanderthal Man buried his dead in specially dug graves and occasionally covered the burial with a slab. Meat was left in some graves (for an after-life?). Sometimes a 'magical' red ochreous powder was sprinkled over the corpse.

Much speculation has gone into Neanderthal Man's way of life or culture which is named the 'Mousterian' culture from an important site called Le Moustier, in France. But it is the origin of this kind of man which causes most discussion. In classification studies we are currently describing ourselves as *Homo sapiens sapiens,* and Neanderthal Man as *Homo sapiens neanderthalensis*. Thus we no longer claim him as a separate species. Some hundreds of thousands of years ago there appeared on the scene an earlier version of ourselves which, while remaining within the definition of *Homo sapiens,* evolved into the Neanderthal man in question. Perhaps it was impossible for modern man to have evolved independently at several places, from a common Neanderthal-like stock. But how can we dare reach complete conclusions when the total finds of early man would barely fill a small lorry?

Mousterian burial

Upper Palaeolithic: Europe, Asia, Africa

For hundreds of thousands of years, man (or a creature very similar to man) made handaxes or produced broad flakes of flint and other stone. Then, in the last glaciation, *Homo sapiens* as we know him today entered Europe. While many workers have argued that *Homo sapiens* moved westwards into Europe, it is still uncertain what cradle-lands made him. But certain facts stand out clear: he had art and was already widespread enough to have many varieties of culture. From about 40,000 to 10,000 B.C., in the last Ice Age, there developed cultures, especially in south-west France, which clearly show that it was in west Europe that the Advanced or Upper Palaeolithic had its finest manifestations. Upper Palaeolithic sites and remains have been found in western Asia and in Africa, and more and more art of that period is being discovered outside western Europe, though the sites in France are those that offer most to an investigator.

Besides art, Upper Palaeolithic cultures offer two new

Advanced Palaeolithic implements; left: from Africa; right: from Siberia

Left: points from the United States; right: from eastern Europe

features: the use of many bone and antler pointed tools, and the manufacture of blade-like flakes which were blanks for making specialized implements for groove-cutting or scraping. Techniques or implements used in later periods were anticipated: the making of baked clay objects; geometrically shaped small implements which were to be so common in the Middle Stone Age; the building of shelters and structures in the open, which were more than mere lean-tos.

Like the Neanderthals, Upper Palaeolithic Man buried his dead. Only now the bodies were flexed (knees to chest), as well as being sprinkled with red ochre. Women were buried with their necklaces and jewellery (made of shells, or animal teeth, or an occasional fossil), together with their babies.

Man was at that time not a savage that instantly attacked other groups. We know this from the fact that men at the end of the Palaeolithic could obtain shells from a sea miles away or bring haematite hundreds of miles to colour beads.

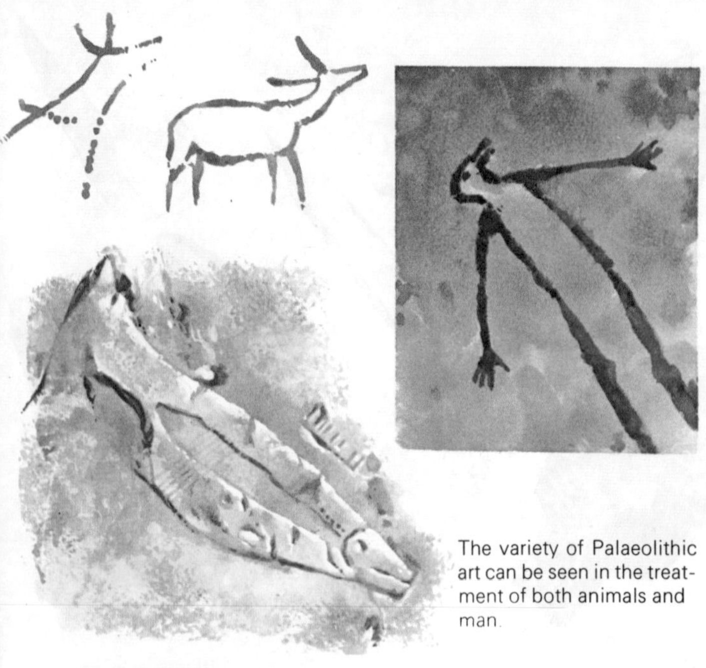

The variety of Palaeolithic art can be seen in the treatment of both animals and man.

Upper Palaeolithic art

In the Upper Palaeolithic Age, particularly man made a cultural leap-forward that still staggers twentieth-century man. In this period, between roughly 30,000 and 8000 B.C. he developed an art of great complexity and variety: paintings and engravings on cave-walls, sculpture in stone, clay, bone and antler. No simple explanation of the motives, both public and individual, of this art can be found.

The lively horses of Lascaux and the powerful bulls of Altamira are too well known to be described here. These are spectacular examples but there is a great quantity of other art which is being studied in increasing detail. The whole phenomenon of Palaeolithic art belongs to the last glaciation and stretches from Portugal to the U.S.S.R., and from Derbyshire in England to Africa. Every year unexpected discoveries are being made.

The drawings themselves tell of the animals that were seen, slain and eaten by Palaeolithic Man: mammoths, elephants, horses, reindeer, salmon, rhinoceros, bison, animals enough

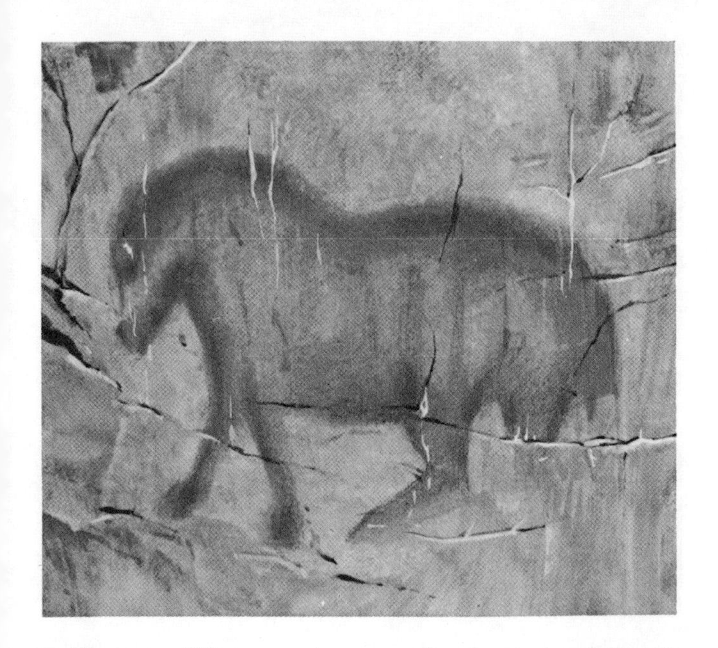

to fill a zoo. Life was not necessarily always harsh but it is difficult to imagine a 'leisured' class of artists indulging in 'art for art's sake'. In trying to understand Palaeolithic art it is foolish to apply twentieth-century ideas about the motivation of art whether they are derived from the sophisticated artists or from the so-called 'primitive' artist. There have been fashions in explaining the art of the Old Stone Age and the archaeologist is cynical about any single explanation for any one human phenomenon. At first it was suggested that the art, which was predominantly about animals, was hunting magic. Man drew the animals he wanted to catch.

Since some of the strange animals shown in cave art are considered either inedible or imaginary, the hunting-magic hypothesis underwent criticism. Others argued that the animals were totem animals. 'Primitive' man does not disengage himself readily from Nature. In addition he can consider animals, trees and stones to be animated as men are. This animism and the totemism which links the identity of

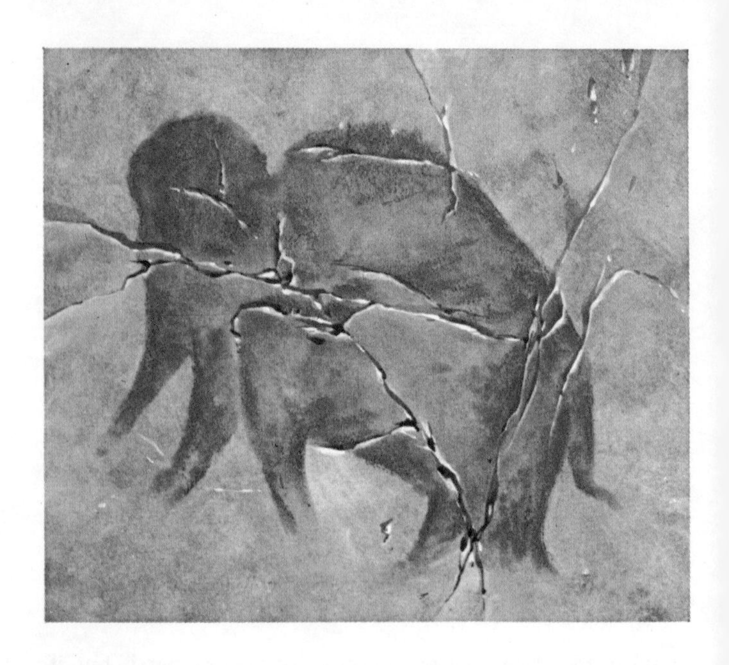

A mammoth. Palaeolithic art from the U.S.S.R.

the individual or the group with an animal or a plant, would lead to representations of the totem and to rituals connected with it. Unfortunately, recent analyses of the relative numbers of species portrayed have made difficulties for those who regard the totem as the main motif.

It is also easy to suggest that cave art was not just decoration. Sometimes drawings were in inaccessible recesses of caves. It is reasonable to suppose that in some cases the drawings could have been for 'initiation' ceremonies.

Another view is that the art is connected with 'fertility', whether of the animals to be hunted or of *Homo sapiens* himself. With growing confidence more and more drawings and symbols have been regarded as relating to sex. There is something in this but many illustrations such as those of a pensive mammoth or a defecating rhinoceros can hardly be described as sexual.

Impression of a hand. Examples of bone carving

While caution is needed, courage is required in visualizing possible explanations. Once it is realized that sometimes the art was created in the context of a mixture of personal and social motives and that, on other occasions the same kind of drawing was initiated at various times and places for completely different motives, then one can return to each painting or group of paintings with more understanding.

Palaeolithic art used many techniques and media: there could be engraving on rock with or without colour. Stone plaques found in one place bore designs of animals in a style found on cave walls miles away: hence the argument for a 'school' of artists. Lamps that lit the artists' work have been found as well as shells full of ochre and other pigments. The paints were charcoal or simple minerals, mixed with water or fats. At some sites evidence of blowpipe spraying of paint has been claimed.

The Upper Palaeolithic

Though in the times when Acheulian handaxes were made or when Mousterian flakes were struck by Neanderthal Man, occasional blades of flint were made into points and knives, it is not until some 40,000 years ago that man appears to acquire a passion for making blade tools. In any blade-making culture one finds the fluted or 'prismatic' cores from which blades have been struck. They vary in dimension from nut-sized to the so-called 'Gigantolith' cores of the Ukraine – a foot long – possibly tools in their own right.

Sometimes the blades were blunted on one edge, just like our steel penknives. Some blades were struck so that the edge planes intersected to provide a sturdy engraving edge; this was the *burin* or *graver*.

Some flints were flaked skilfully until the parallel scars produced flutings side by side, that make one end like the cow-catcher of an old locomotive. This is called a *plane*. Certain cultures of the Upper Palaeolithic such as the Solutrian made exceptionally thin leaf-shaped spearheads or knives.

Burins were the tools that were used to draw outlines of animal shapes or to carve or decorate bone objects. These blade-derived tools were used to make a distinctive implement, the bone or reindeer antler point. Needles of bone became common in the later part of the Upper Palaeolithic.

One characteristic piece of Advanced Palaeolithic equipment is the spear thrower, used as an extension of the arm.

By the end of the 1960s it became possible to assemble a broad view of the Upper Palaeolithic from Wales to Japan. This period which ranges, according to current estimates, from 40,000 B.C. to about 10,000 B.C. offers a variety of cultures that show how complex man's life was then. Even without the evidence of skilfully made tools or of Ice Age art, we would still be impressed by the traces of huts or tent bases found in the U.S.S.R., France and elsewhere.

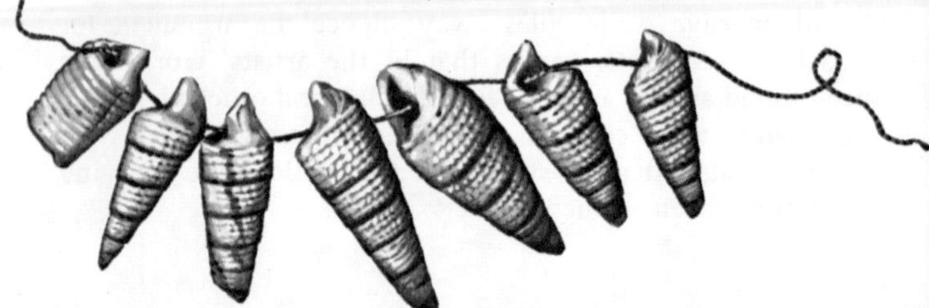

One of the great perils in trying to reconstruct prehistory is our use of modern parallels. Note that the figure is not meant to represent an Eskimo.

The spread of Upper Palaeolithic cultures

In the last glaciation in Asia and Europe it is possible to discern at many sites the contrast, with some overlaps, between the sequence of Mousterian flakes and the blades of Upper Palaeolithic man. In an inter-stadial or warm phase of the last glaciation there may have arisen just the right conditions for modern man to develop new techniques or ways of life. Already in Hungary, Austria, Poland, Rumania, the Ukraine and elsewhere a culture called the *Szeletian*– which is post-Mousterian – was producing leaf-shaped spear-heads or points with a new technique. Then, over, 30,000 years ago appears more certainly modern *Homo sapiens* with his blades and bone points. He did not originate in Western Europe and we are still not certain as to where he came from. Guesses that it was from Palestine or beyond the Caucasus are of little help.

The cultures of the Upper Palaeolithic have been best studied in France where they are at their richest. But their distribution goes deep into Western Asia.

In France various workers have distinguished a *Perigordian* stage with blunted-back blades and points, some burins, and some broad flakes like Mousterian scrapers.

Following this there is the *Aurignacian* culture which is

Artist's reconstruction of a Palaeolithic tent

Burials are sometimes the only evidence we have of prehistoric culture

largely independent of the Perigordian. Aurignacian tool kits include split-base spear points of bone, end-scrapers, chunky burins and nosed scrapers made from half a pebble. Implements of similar types have often been found in Asia and elsewhere and the label 'Aurignacian' has been often too freely conferred.

In France and elsewhere there then intruded a culture called the *Solutrian* with its characteristic leaf-shaped points which, like bone needles, supplemented a normal Upper Palaeolithic equipment.

Then there arose the richest and most varied of the European cultures of the Upper Palaeolithic, the *Magdalenian,* best known for its harpoons with twin runs of curved barbs, and a great variety of stone implements, many of them displaying great skill in producing a vast system of burins, tanged points and tiny borers, and quite a few small items that are precursors of the small flints or microliths of the

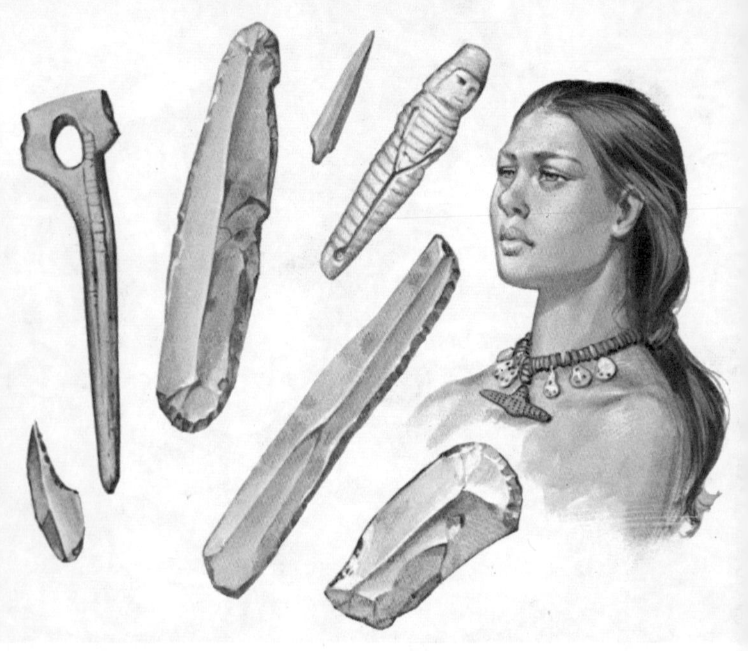

Palaeolithic flints and beads from Eastern Europe and central Asia

post-glacial Middle Stone Age, or Mesolithic period.

The Magdalenian is largely a Western European culture but parallels are found as far as Siberia.

Similar cultures do not occur in, say, China or India; so often there seems a gap between the chunkier Lower Palaeolithic items and the tiny microliths of the Mesolithic. But not every part of the world has been archaeologically explored.

Some late Palaeolithic cultures outside Europe

In Africa there is no Upper Palaeolithic tradition like those of the Aurignacian or Magdalenian of Europe. But in North West Africa and Kenya, *Homo sapiens* of the 'Capsian' culture made stone blades and burins together with small flints belonging more in style to the late Mesolithic. Moreover the Capsian (c. 6000 B.C.) and an earlier culture of about 10,000 B.C. and later from Morocco, Spain and elsewhere called the Iberomaurusian which had tiny blades and points, are of the very end of the Pleistocene and much later than the allegedly similar cultures of Europe. So in Africa one speaks of a Middle Stone Age which bridges the gap between the Palaeolithic and the Neolithic. Many African Middle Stone Age cultures persist until quite late and some of them use pottery.

In India and China there is again a very poor display of cultures that might be considered a bridge between the Palaeolithic and the flints of a post-glacial hunting cultures. In several parts of India blade industries or cultures have occasionally turned up. They are not very plentiful and they were followed by a rich variety of cultures employing small stone tools, numerous examples of which have been found in recent years.

In North China, as at Sjara-osso-gol, in Suiyuan in the great curve of the Yellow river, remains of a culture have been found over a hundred feet below ground. The assemblage discovered has blades and burins plus tiny bladelets that would not be dissimilar to Magdalenian ones from Europe. The Sjara-osso-gol finds are of a warm phase of the last glaciation, but few would confidently date these items. There is an earlier stone industry from Shui-tung-kou, also in Suiyuan, where blades were found with tools looking like Mousterian flakes. A date between 50,000 and 10,000 B.C. is the best that can be given at the moment with our present state of knowledge.

From Siberia there is an odd variation of the familiar pattern. There is an Upper Palaeolithic like that of Europe which has many features in common with that of Europe: blades, female figurines, bone implements and the like. One interesting feature is the use of huts or pit houses: the Siberian Upper Palaeolithic was sometimes sedentary. Later the same period saw an astonishing change: tools became crude and sometimes resembled the pebble tools of early man. In contrast the antler and bone harpoons were developed and cultures came into being which have much in common with some Eskimo cultures.

The story of man's progress has had many reverses during the course of time: archaeology reminds us that there could be halts in 'progress' at any stage.

The end of the Ice Age

Around 12,000–10,000 B.C., the ice that capped the northern hemisphere (as well as the Antarctic regions) began to retreat. The enormous quantities of water ponded up as ice returned to the sea and the sea-level rose. Areas such as Britain or Scandinavia, which had been under the weight of ice for thousands of years began to rise out of the sea and partly cancelled the effect of the rising sea. Some land bridges were broken or uncovered. Australia and America were possibly linked with parts of Asia around this time – though precise dates are difficult to produce.

The general climate of Europe and even its prevailing winds altered. Some animals adapted to warm climates, others such as the mammoth or the reindeer disappeared or moved north. Some men may have found this distressing and instead of basking in the temperate climes moved north after the animals they knew so well. In French sites such as Mas d'Azil the barbed harpoons of reindeer antler are no longer to be found; instead red deer antler is used.

Perhaps the most significant change is in the vegetation. Archaeologists and botanists have learnt much from seeing in excavations the successive layers containing pollen and plant remains which begin in the lower levels with the flora of a chilly, tundra-like environment not far from the ice-face. Plants like the dwarf-willow prevail at first and slowly over eight thousand years each vegetation climax is reached and passed. There were times when the elm is more plentiful and flourishing in Europe than it is now; at other times the climate is not so helpful. Besides fluctuations and climaxes there were several minor variations in the sea-level such as the ones that flooded the fenlands which are now the North Sea or broke through to separate England from France.

Pollen survives astonishingly well over thousands of years. Left to right: oak, beech, pine, hazel, birch.

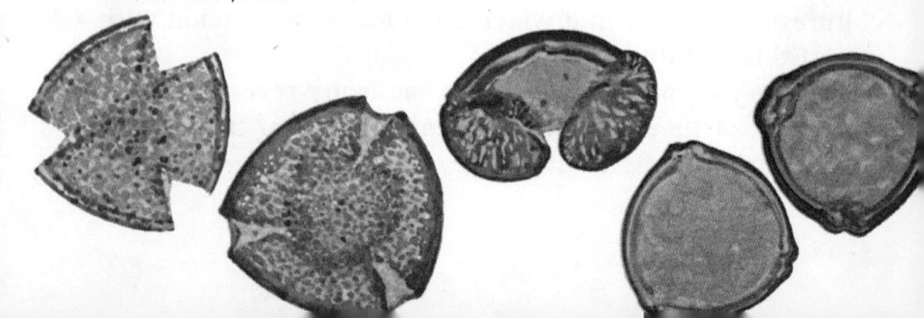

Sub-Atlantic (c. 500 B.C.+)
cooler and wetter
birch and beech increase

Sub-Boreal (2500–c. 500 B.C.)
drier
increase in birch ; less hazel

Atlantic (5000–2500 B.C.)
warm and moist
mixed : oak, elm, lime, hazel, alder

Boreal (7000–5000 B.C.)
dry, a little warmer
pine and hazel, varying

Pre-Boreal
coldish (before 7000 B.C.)
dwarf willow, tundra plants

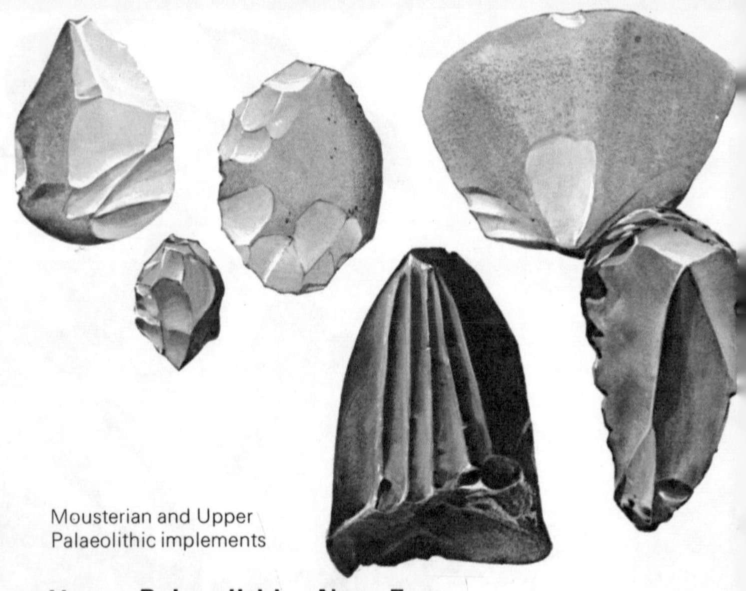

Mousterian and Upper Palaeolithic implements

Upper Palaeolithic: Near East

In Europe there were many 'Mousterian' cultures which were followed by Upper Palaeolithic cultures. In the Near East and North Africa the picture is complicated by the presence at the end of the Pleistocene (see pp. 8–9) of cultures which are a hybrid of the Mousterian and the earlier Levalloisian 'flakes-from-prepared-cores' cultures: hence the bewildering term Levalloiso-Mousterian.

In Palestine, at Mount Carmel, blades (like Upper Palaeolithic types) have been found in late Acheulian (handaxes) deposits. Similarly, the roughly contemporary Levalloiso-Mousterian flake-industries of the Near East and North Africa have blades – and, more important, the human remains resemble those of modern man. Here is the exciting nub of a great problem: when and where did modern *Homo sapiens* develop? What was his culture and environment? Some answers, but only partial ones may emerge before these pages are printed. There are not enough sites investigated and it would be naive to expect that the origins of Upper Palaeolithic Man will be found exclusively in the areas bounding the south eastern coasts of the Mediterranean.

It is possible, as often is the case in archaeology, that blade cultures developed out of 'Mousterian' cultures independently. The Shanidar Cave, after being deserted by its 'Mousterian' (Neanderthal) occupants, was left unoccupied for ten thousand years before the blade-makers came in. The reader should also be reminded at this point that *it is assumed* that the makers of blades were of modern *Homo sapiens;* many stone finds have no skeletons to go with them. It may seem that too much space has been given in this booklet to the cultures of the tail-end of the Ice Age. It is a necessary emphasis since it is easy for author and reader to gravitate to the more spectacular archaeology of great civilizations where events and sequences are easier to grasp. But the techniques of interpretations used for the Upper Palaeolithic, are the best training for the would-be archaeologist. This kind of work is mentally tough and is more demanding than the archaeology of other periods since the prehistorian has to be an authority on the typology of implements and an expert on environment and skeletal finds.

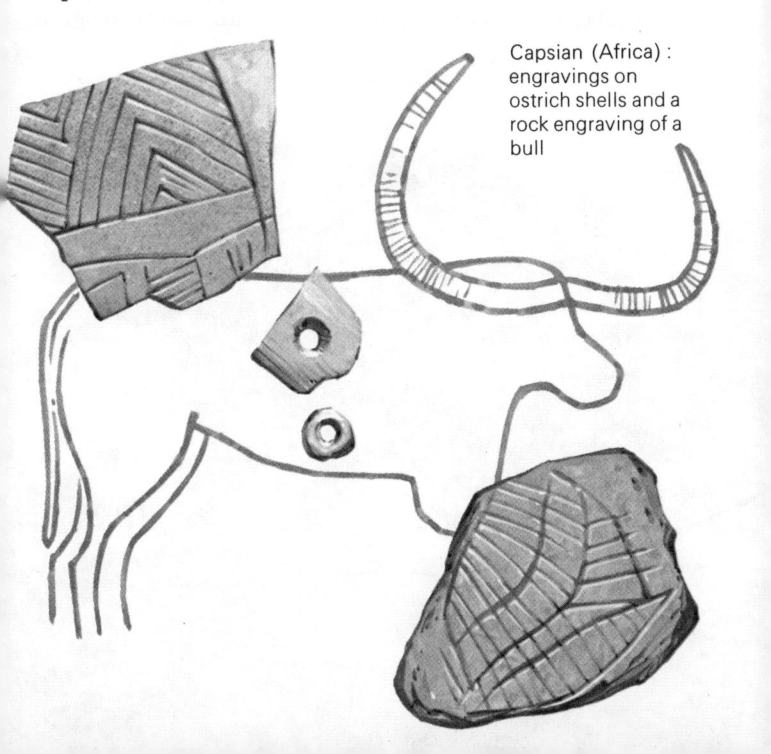

Capsian (Africa): engravings on ostrich shells and a rock engraving of a bull

Typology

The person who is being introduced to archaeology for the first time, and has read so far may be a little restive by now. So many cultures, so many blade types, so many 'fore-shadowings of the Mesolithic' and the like may make him feel that we have gone too far from people with hands, eyes, noses and ears, who grapple daily with their environment. But the archaeologist is duty-bound to carry out enquiries as to the *dates* of things and their *origins* and *influences*. Dating by physical or chemical methods works only in certain circumstances and the archaeologist has often to rely on *typology*: 'This object is of a type usually found in the Upper Palaeolithic. There being no other aspects of the context to cause doubts on the matter, we say that this object is of an Upper Palaeolithic type, and therefore, of the Upper Palaeolithic period.' This is in many respects a very sensible thing to do. One can date an old car roughly, or sometimes quite accurately, because it is a 'pre-war type' or that it is a 'red label pre-1933 type', and so on. With cars typology is

The numbers indicate where the objects on the opposite page were found.

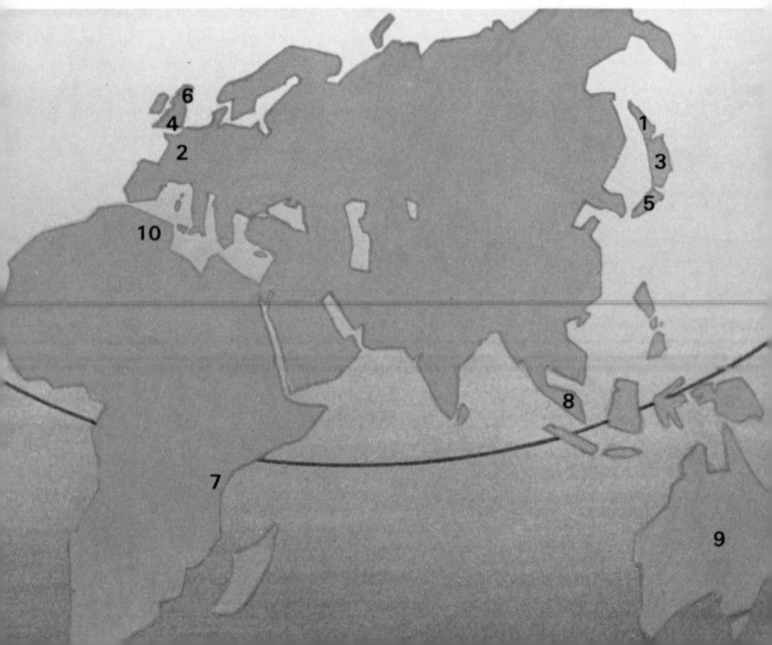

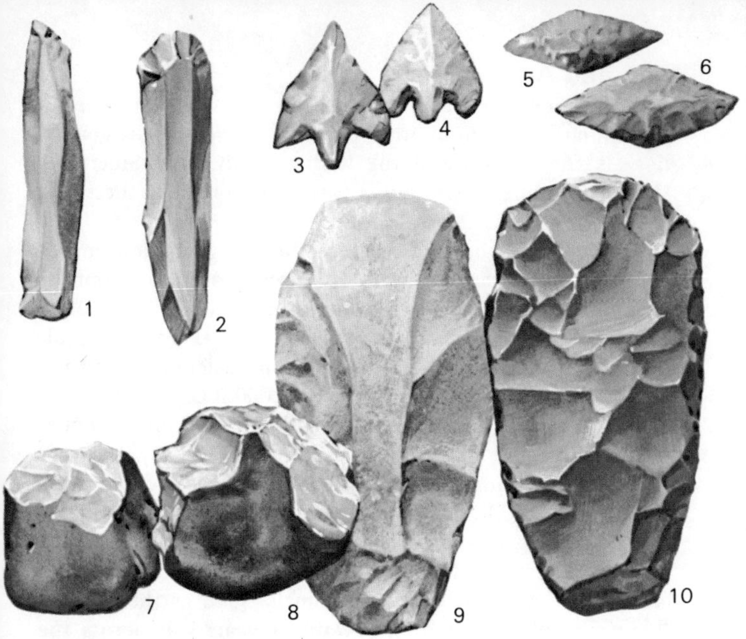

Typology can prove links, but it can mislead us with apparent similarities.

all right, but man has archaizing tendencies, frequently introducing 'reproductions' or imitations of 'vintage models'.

The flint blade which is the 'typical' tool of the Upper Palaeolithic of the last glaciation, was also made thousands of years before in the Acheulian. Blades were used thousands of years after the Palaeolithic in the Neolithic, from Siberia to England. But the *frequency* of blades not from the Upper Palaeolithic is much less.

Similarly an archaeologist may find a flint flake made from a carefully prepared core which was so chipped that if tapped at one point it would release a wide but thin flake which is just the shape the maker visualized. This technique is named the Levallois technique – after a place near Paris where these flakes (and their cores) were first recognized. The Levallois *culture* is thought to date to the glaciation before the last one, and to the warm interglacial period that preceeded the last glaciation. But the technique continued into the last glaciation.

Man and America

As far as one can tell, man came on the scene in America very much later than in other parts of the world. The general view is that he crossed the Bering Strait from Siberia to Alaska, at a time when the sea was lower, or when there was an ice bridge.

The migrants got across before the last glaciation ended, and many American archaeologists are prepared to accept the possibility that there were game hunters where the United States are now even as early as 30,000 B.C. Most reliable radiocarbon datings from sites with implements still do not put the evidence much earlier than 20,000 B.C., but there are many excavated examples of mammoth and other bones found with lance-like projectile points of stone, which are shouldered or fluted at the base. Most of these finds (from 13,000–5000 B.C.) are from western North America and the plains, and Mexico and parts of South America.

As the ice retreated and the climate grew drier and warmer, man learned to hunt different animals, such as the buffalo. There may also have been several new arrivals across the Bering Strait. By 5000 B.C., or even a few thousand years earlier, seed collection became a major source of food, though hunting was rarely neglected.

The cultivation of plants seems to have been developed at three or more centres. In Mexico, and just over the border, around 6000 B.C. the squash and possibly other vegetables were already being cultivated. Beans, and then maize, followed between 5000 and 2000 B.C., perhaps beaten to the post as a cereal by foxtail millet. A little later than in Mexico, in Venezuela, Peru and the Amazon area, root plants like manioc were among the first which were to be cultivated in South America.

Pottery appeared before 2500 B.C. in both Central and South America, and by 1000 B.C. there were places in many parts of the continent that could be termed towns. All this was developed, as far as we know, without any contact with the Old World, though there are vigorous attempts made periodically to show trans-Pacific linkages with the Far East.

Coyote head from llama bone; typical local stone points

Left: axe from France.
Right: various microliths.
Below: 'pick' from Spain.

Mesolithic cultures

The archaeologist faced by the complexity and variety of human cultures even ten or five thousand years ago, yearns to be able to label or classify his discoveries and then to make meaningful comparisons. The Palaeolithic from the time of the handaxes to that of the Upper Palaeolithic blades and harpoons is clear; so is the later New Stone Age, with its polished axes. Before the 1880s the contrast between the Palaeolithic and the Neolithic was found so obvious that an 'in between' (or middle) Stone Age, the Mesolithic, was postulated for certain finds.

Pygmy flints, later called 'microliths', and waste items from their making to be found in many parts of the world, came to be recognized as distinctive of the cultures that man adopted as a hunter and food gatherer after the ice had retreated around 10,000 B.C. The tundra, or woodland, or fenland Mesolithic cultures of Northern Europe and Asia which had axes or picks as well as microliths, were well studied before 1914, but there was much uncertainty as to what 'Mesolithic' cultures there were in more southern climes, in South-West Asia or North Africa.

These questions are not irrelevant in discussions about man's cultural evolution, but they led to extremes such as when there is no Mesolithic but a proto or pre-Neolithic. Indeed some of the key features of the Neolithic have occurred in Mesolithic cultures. To make matters worse, cultures were found in North Germany and elsewhere which looked too late to be Palaeolithic and yet did not have enough Mesolithic features to be called Mesolithic.

Yet there are many contrasts and overlaps between Palaeolithic, Mesolithic and Neolithic cultures, especially in the Near East that it would be naive to refuse to classify. Often, as with the proto-Neolithic Natufian (Palestine) of the earlier Neolithic of Shanidar (Iraq) it is possible to see some features common with the Upper Palaeolithic. In addition, the Natufian has offered evidence of sickles with the gloss obtained in cutting uncultivated cereals.

It is becoming clearer that there are some areas which have not gone through the Mesolithic stage. In Southern Africa a 'Late Stone Age' survived until the African Iron Age.

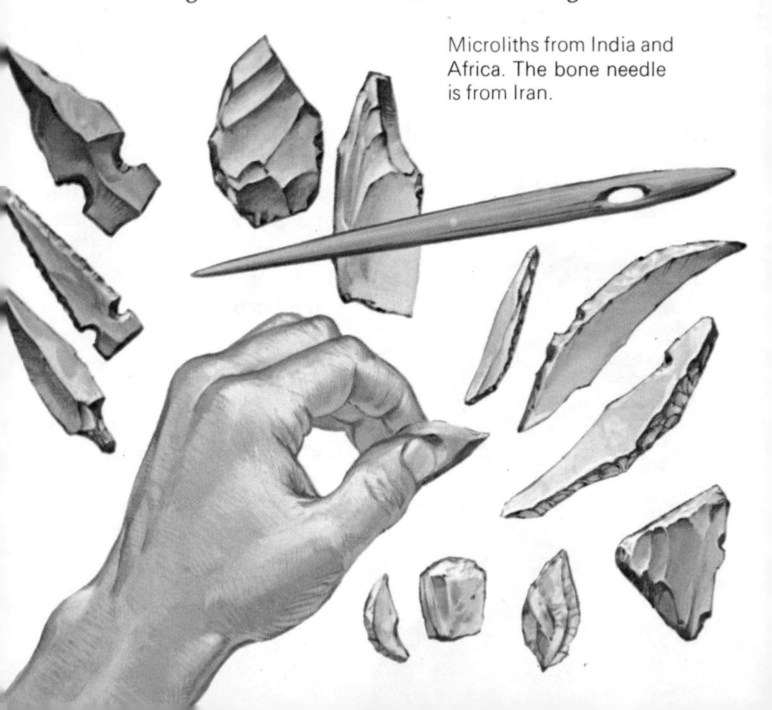

Microliths from India and Africa. The bone needle is from Iran.

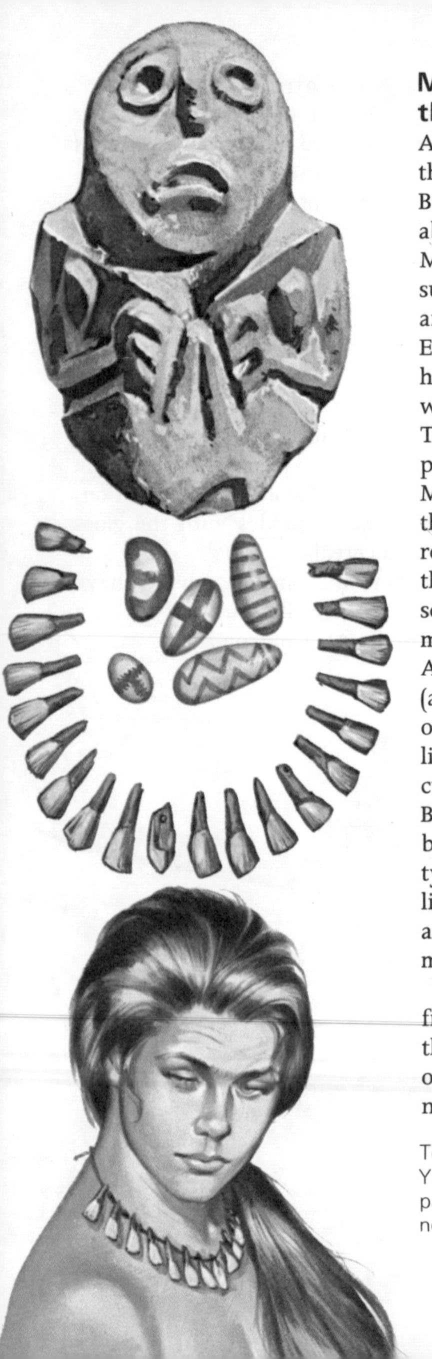

Mesolithic cultures of the North

As pointed out, the end of the Ice Age about 10,000 B.C. did not produce an abrupt change of equipment. Many Mesolithic cultures such as the Azilian of France and Spain, and the North European Ahrensburgian have features in common with the Upper Palaeolithic. The Azilian has barbed harpoons like those of the Magdalenian, but this time they are of red deer, not reindeer. The mighty art of the Palaeolithic is sometimes seen to survive as reddish marks on pebbles. The Ahrensburgians who lived (about 8500 B.C.) in tents all over the European plain, had, like the Polish Swiderian cultures of about 10,000 B.C. and later, blades and burins of Upper Palaeolithic type and a few small microliths (small flints slotted into arrow or harpoon shafts to make barbs or 'teeth').

In the north of Europe from the Baltic to Britain there was an environment of trees, meres and fens. It is not surprising that the

Top: Mesolithic carving, Yugoslavia. Centre: Azilian painted pebbles, and stag-tooth necklace, Poland.

cultures found a living hunting, fowling and fruit-gathering used the bow, and axes with broad cutting edges. At times there were axes of antler and various experiments were tried in tool making. Sometimes flint axes were hafted in antler sleeves.

The Tardenoisian culture, noted in France and further east, with its triangular and trapeze-like microliths, was already in touch with Neolithic folk. It was more advanced than the earlier Sauveterrian with pointed flakes which have been found in Britain, France and elsewhere.

Another Mesolithic culture whose dumps of shells in Denmark and Germany gave it its nickname of 'Kitchen-midden folk' was that of Ertebølle; a few pots found their way into their chattels.

Each region has its own post-glacial Mesolithic culture – the coasts of, for example, Ireland, Scotland, Norway, Spain and Portugal produce rough stone tools which do not have microliths but are definitely Mesolithic in date.

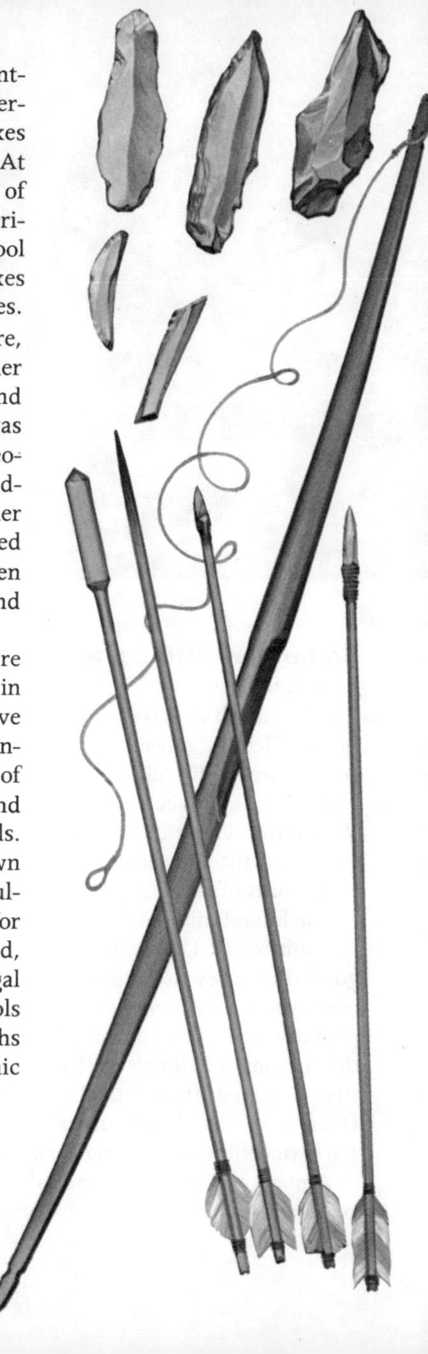

Natufian flints and Danish bow and arrows.

A northern Mesolithic side

Some Mesolithic sites

Star Carr

There is such a variety in the post-glacial sites which could be labelled as 'Mesolithic' that it will only be possible to select two well-studied excavations which each offer both extremes and overlaps. One is in England, at Star Carr, in Yorkshire, where in the eighth millennium B.C. small groups of Mesolithic hunters and food gatherers were squatters on a platform of birch stems by a reed-bordered lake.

The inhabitants settled at this spot sporadically, and only in late winter and early spring, but they seem to have had a good diet: they ate red and roe deer, elk, ox, pig and plant items such as the yellow water lily, and bog beans.

Many small (microlithic) flint arrowheads were found and this is some evidence of the use of the bow. The other flint items ranged from burins and scrapers to the occasional flake axe. Red deer antler was used for making barbed harpoon points or fishing-fork prongs.

Among the items of special interest were a wood canoe paddle, fragments of birch-bark containers, a pyrites fire-striker and fungus tinder. The life at Star Carr is regarded as being an early example of the Maglemosian culture that spread between the Baltic and Western England.

The Belt Cave

The Belt Cave (or Ghar-i-Kamarband, the Cave of the 'Cummerbund') is by the shores of the Caspian in Iran, and is as far as possible from Star Carr in place and context. The excavators got down through to the base levels of this cave, and of the nearby Hotu Cave. Near the bottom was an early Mesolithic site of around 9500 B.C. when the glaciations were coming to an end in the north. These Mesolithic people hunted seals with bow and arrow and, in addition, are thought to have had the dog as a domesticated animal assistant. Around 6600 B.C. the people of this cave hunted a species of gazelle and a thousand years later they were Neolithic, bringing in pottery within a few hundred years.

Sites like Belt and Hotu never give a complete sequence from the Mesolithic to the full Neolithic but they help produce a useful, tentative picture.

Excavating in the Ghar-i-Kamarband cave in Iran

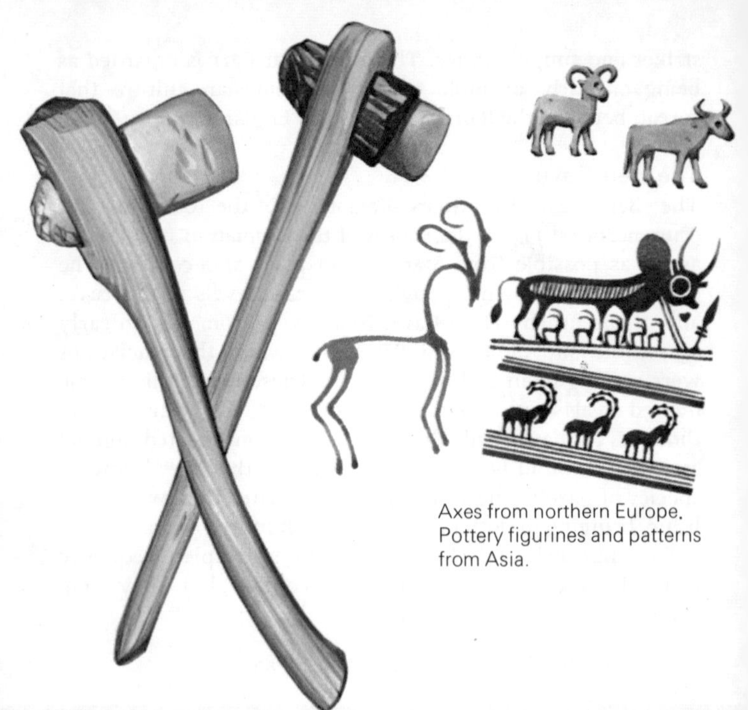

Axes from northern Europe. Pottery figurines and patterns from Asia.

The first farmers

The word 'Neolithic', which refers to the 'New Stone' Age, has been in use for a hundred years. The word was originally used to label the polished stone axes which have been found in all the continents of the world. Later it was grasped that the users of polished axes were first users of pots and, eventually it was realized that Neolithic peoples were the first to domesticate animals and to cultivate plants. These last two features are the important ones for stone tools seem to have been polished in both the Palaeolithic and the Bronze Age!

The change to a Neolithic way of life was a startling one since man changed from being a food gatherer or a hunter to being a *food producer*. This means that instead of a large area (even a hundred square miles or more) maintaining a few persons, a relatively small area of cultivated land and pasture can maintain hundreds of people. These are perhaps too easy generalizations. Not all peoples became sedentary after the Neolithic. While no one doubts the radical changes that the Neolithic brought into man's life, it was a gradual process rather than a sharp revolution. Nor did pottery, domestic animals, cultivated plants and polished axes appear on the same day! In some areas, such as Jericho, there was 'pre-pottery Neolithic'. It is possible too that even in the Mesolithic there was some domestication of animals, but that did not add up to a Neolithic. In Denmark some food-gathering folk used or made pots; the general view is that they picked up the idea from Neolithic neighbours, but again this does not mean that they were at a Neolithic stage.

The beginner should give much thought to this step in the evolution of man's culture. The study of the Neolithic is the key to much in the study of human society and its environment. The important thing for the beginner to grasp is that the Neolithic did not take place at one time and that it did not begin at any one centre. Some peoples, like the Australian Aborigines, never reached the Neolithic stage.

Pottery: top, from Hacilar; middle and bottom from Siyalk

Man and animals

Archaeologists often find animal bones in prehistoric and historic sites. It is not enough to record types and numbers of bones, and stop at that since an enormous amount of interpretation is required. Are the bones of domestic or wild animals? Is the presence of bones accidental, or ritual, or evidence of diet? Or all three?

It is difficult to work out whether a sheep's remains are of a domesticated animal except by careful analysis of the bones. There are times when it is difficult to distinguish a sheep's

Above: early sheep. Below: an early domestic dog.

bone from a goat's. Very often the only clue about domestication comes from prehistoric models in clay.

In some deposits animal and mollusc remains are an indication of climate. A turtle or a shellfish may indicate a warmer or a colder climate. Bones of an elk, a lemming, a polar bear or a mammoth indicate a cold climate, while monkey, pig, antelope and vole bones help indicate mild conditions. The archaeologist who is incurious about animals is at a disadvantage. He should at least, be able to recognize whether a rabbit or a mole has disturbed a layer.

It is possible that in the Neolithic and later, man learned more than once to domesticate a particular species of animal. The pig and the dog are examples of animals that were domesticated in different places at different times. It is hard to say which animal was the first to join man. Sheep, goats and pigs began to be controlled by man in the Near East before 6000 B.C. roughly at the same time as full-scale plant cultivation began. Some workers claim that there is strong evidence from Shanidar in North Iraq that the sheep was domesticated by 9000 B.C.

By 6000 B.C. there were domesticated cattle browsing in Anatolia or elsewhere. Whether these were the first domesticated breeds, only future excavations can tell us. The dog is thought to have been domesticated in the Mesolithic – but there is always the problem of distinguishing the bones of these animals from those of foxes and wolves.

Wild ancestors of modern domesticated animals

Early grain types
and flint sickle

Man and plants

While it is easy to grasp what plant cultivation implies – the saving of seed and the working of thc soil, together with knowledge of seed propagation – the story of how man in the Old and the New World learned to cultivate and select plants for breeding is far from clear.

The archaeologist finds evidence of grains which are larger than the wild variety; he also finds sickles and possibly objects that might be taken for hoes. It is possible the sickles might have been used for gathering wild plants. If the grains or fruit are of a plant species which is consistently larger than the wild variety then we are on the way to recognizing plant remains as cultivated. But size is not the main indication: some of the first Neolithic farmers and horticulturalists may have selected small plants for their power to survive bad weather conditions – or for their flavour or for their ability to hold out against the competition of weeds, or even conceivably, for some feature such as colour that was important for magic. There are many cases where it may be said that plants cultivated man.

When and where were the first plants cultivated or domesticated? From the evidence at the time of writing it seems likely that by 9000–8000 B.C. which is not long

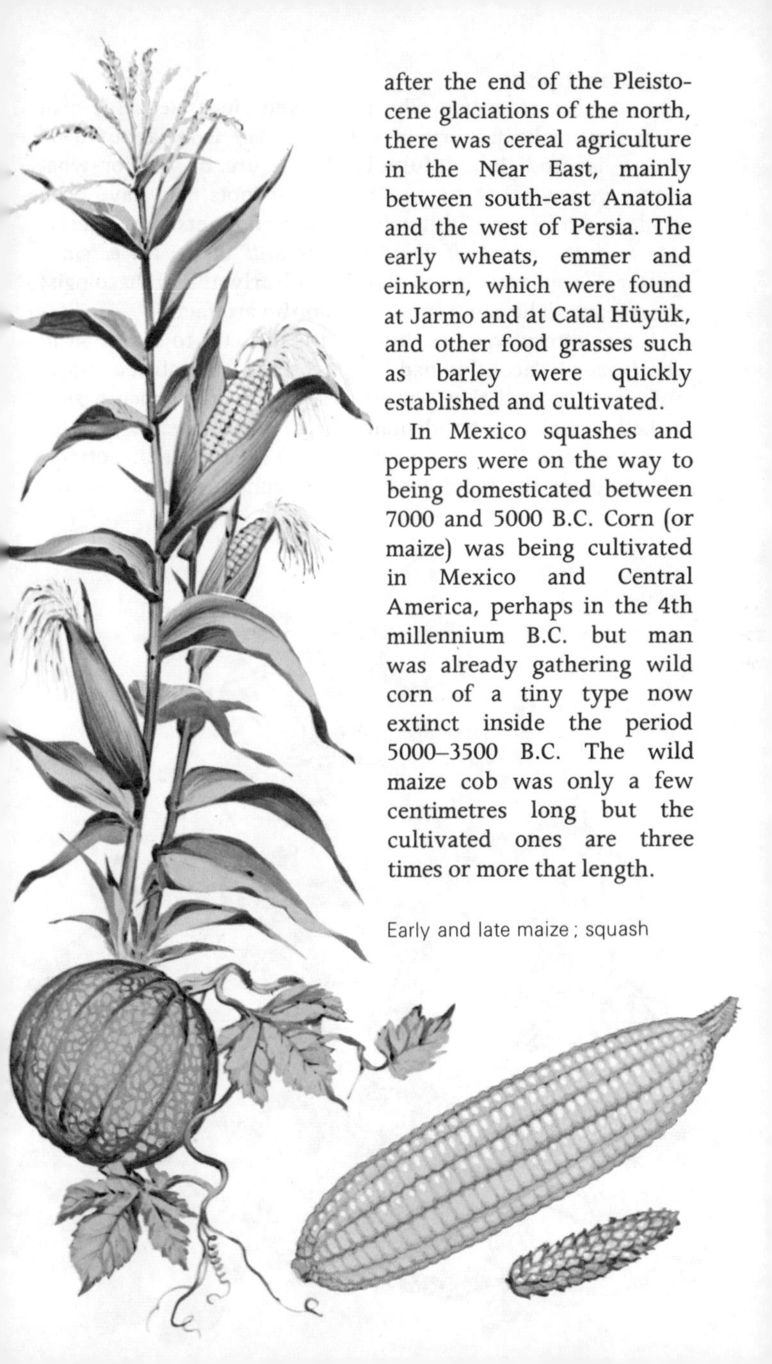

after the end of the Pleistocene glaciations of the north, there was cereal agriculture in the Near East, mainly between south-east Anatolia and the west of Persia. The early wheats, emmer and einkorn, which were found at Jarmo and at Catal Hüyük, and other food grasses such as barley were quickly established and cultivated.

In Mexico squashes and peppers were on the way to being domesticated between 7000 and 5000 B.C. Corn (or maize) was being cultivated in Mexico and Central America, perhaps in the 4th millennium B.C. but man was already gathering wild corn of a tiny type now extinct inside the period 5000–3500 B.C. The wild maize cob was only a few centimetres long but the cultivated ones are three times or more that length.

Early and late maize; squash

Man and pots

The number of people who have lived since Neolithic man began to make pottery in earnest – say from about 6500 B.C. – is prodigious. Multiply that figure by ten (or what figure you wish) to suggest how many pots may have been made and a figure with twelve or more noughts may emerge. *Most of the fabric of these pots is still in existence,* since pottery fragments are so durable. Clearly the archaeologist must learn all he can from so common an artefact.

How pottery was first invented is difficult to say. Man in the Upper Palaeolithic had learnt to bake clay objects. Some folk have argued that pottery was discovered when a sun-baked vessel was accidentally fired, but evidence for this is not easy to find. It is probably more certain that pottery, allowing for the helpful social and economic climate of the

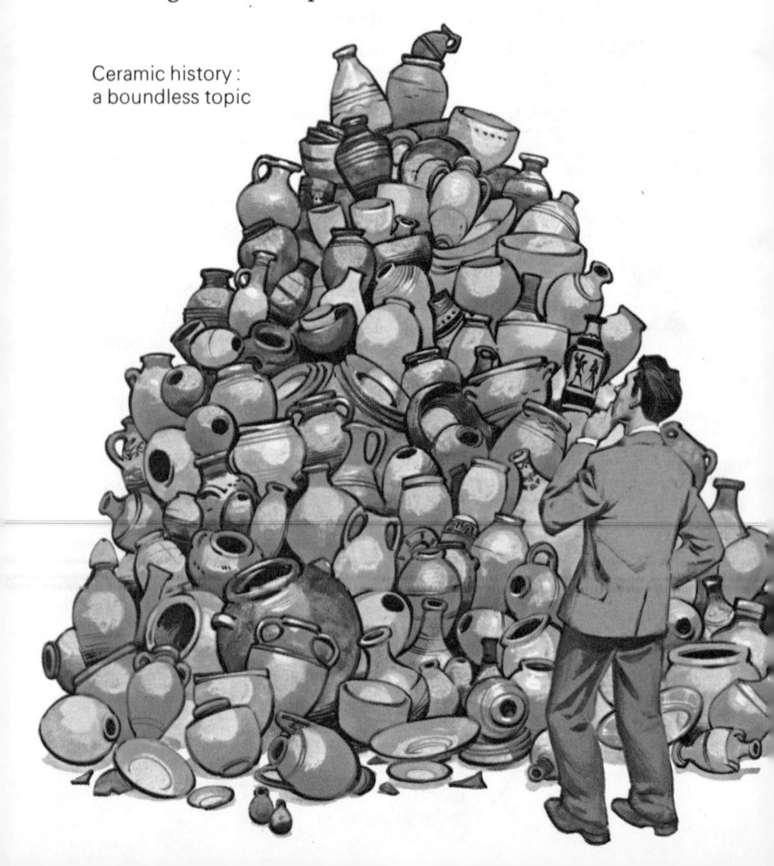

Ceramic history: a boundless topic

Neolithic pottery. Upper left from Spain, upper right from Yugoslavia, lower left from China, lower right from Turkey.

Neolithic, could be invented several times in the sedentary conditions possible at the time. Some early vessels may have been sun-dried. Most scholars are prepared to accept that pottery was independently invented in America some time after 3000 B.C. The change it brought into man's life is indubitable. Soup and beer became possible for the first time.

The archaeologist has to be aware that some peoples can cease to make pottery. This has happened not only in the isles of the Pacific but, according to some accounts, in medieval Scotland and in pre-colonial Africa, and elsewhere. Wood, leather, horn, stone and, later, metal vessels may have been used at certain times.

A good archaeologist must be familiar with the basic techniques of potting: he should, for example, understand the methods by which pottery was made without a wheel – as it always was in ancient America. A potter's wheel of some sort or other was in use in Mesopotamia between 3500 and 3000 B.C. The potter's wheel came into Britain just before the Romans came. In Saxon times pots were again made without the wheel. Techniques seem to come and go and return.

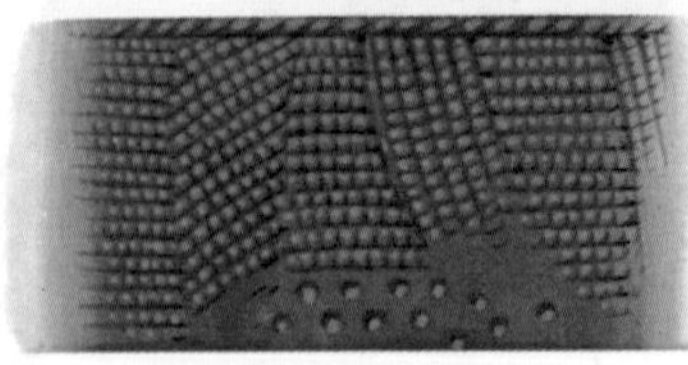

Neolithic pottery details. Top : Hacilar and Thessaly. Centre : India. Bottom : Kenya.

Neolithic life

The word Stone Age gives the man in the street, the idea of a 'primitive' world in a state of barbarism. It is important therefore to show that Neolithic (or New Stone Age) Man was sometimes more than a primitive agriculturist and pastoralist who happened also to have pots. We must also recall that the Neolithic lasted in some areas five or more thousand years.

First, Neolithic Man was a clever craftsman. He was, for example, a great carpenter and could, even with stone tools, make planks with dowel holes in them. He, or his womenfolk, could weave clothes and stitch them together, as well as make baskets and mats. Many other techniques were at his disposal, though evidence for this is uncertain. For example, the cereals that came into his diet may have made him appreciate salt. Some archaeologists have been investigating the possibility that salt was used as an object of 'trade'.

Perhaps the most unusual aspect of the skills of Neolithic Man was his practicality as a geological prospector. In Britain, for example, he learned to mine with antler picks through chalk to get at high grade flints. But this is not his only skill. In an island off Northern Ireland there is an isolated spot where there is a small vein of hard blue-grey rock. Some Neolithic prospector learned to ferret this out and to quarry this hard stone for ultimate manufacture as polished axes – one of which was traded as far as the Thames Valley. How the stone was shipped it is hard to say, but Neolithic ships, must have been seaworthy vessels to enable Britain and Ireland to be 'colonized' in the first place.

Early Neolithic Man built cities and could be adept at walled town defences. In some lands he produced a lively art, especially clay figurines of deities or animals.

While places like Jericho and Catal Hüyük are recognized as spectacular Asian examples of urban cultures (Neolithic Man 'invented' cities) it is possible that great Neolithic towns may yet be found in Europe and elsewhere.

In a way too, it can be said that Neolithic Man discovered the use of metal and thus created the age of metal. Perhaps it will be feasible one day to show that writing was first devised in the Neolithic of more than one land.

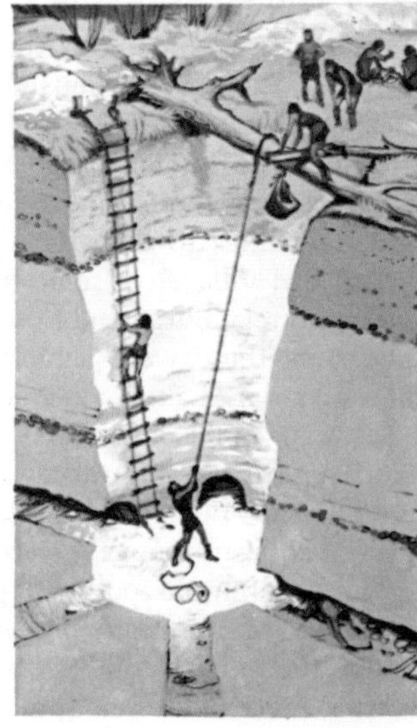

Axe rough-out, Wales. Textile, Hacilar. Flint mine England.

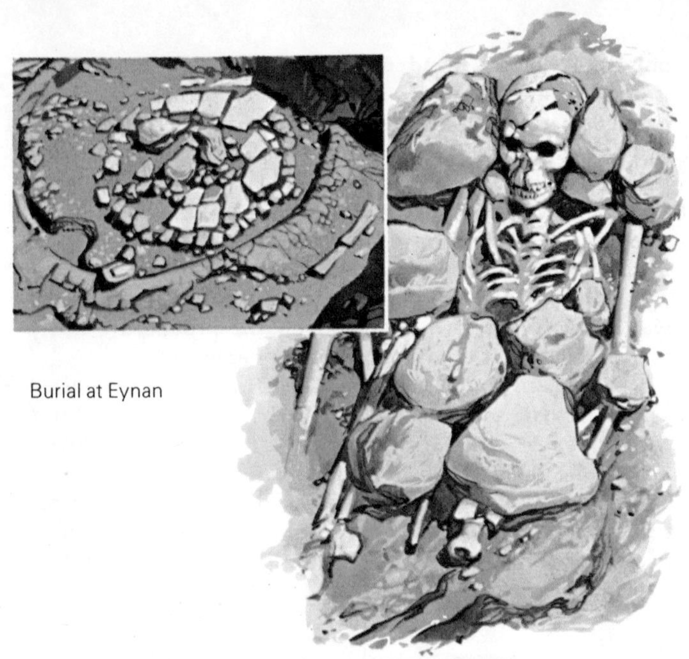

Burial at Eynan

The Early Neolithic in the Near East

The Proto-Neolithic in the Near East is regarded as beginning about 9000 B.C. What and where was this Proto-Neolithic? There are many examples and one may cite the Natufians of Palestine who hunted gazelles and other animals but had a taste for a cereal diet and used small flints mounted as teeth in bone sickles to reap food plants. Some Natufians (as at Eynan) had villages of some fifty stone-walled houses. They had no pottery but already they had stone pots. At about the same time there were similar Proto-Neolithic cultures 500 miles away at Shanidar in Iraq.

Between 8000 and 7000 B.C. a development of the Natufian culture produced a town of some 10 acres at Jericho. The houses were neatly made of mud bricks and the 'city' walls and towers were of stone. Jericho then had agriculture but no pottery; gazelle-hunting was the main source of protein rather than cattle-keeping. Few would grudge the term 'Neolithic' to Jericho.

After 7000 B.C. a new (pre-pottery) Neolithic culture took

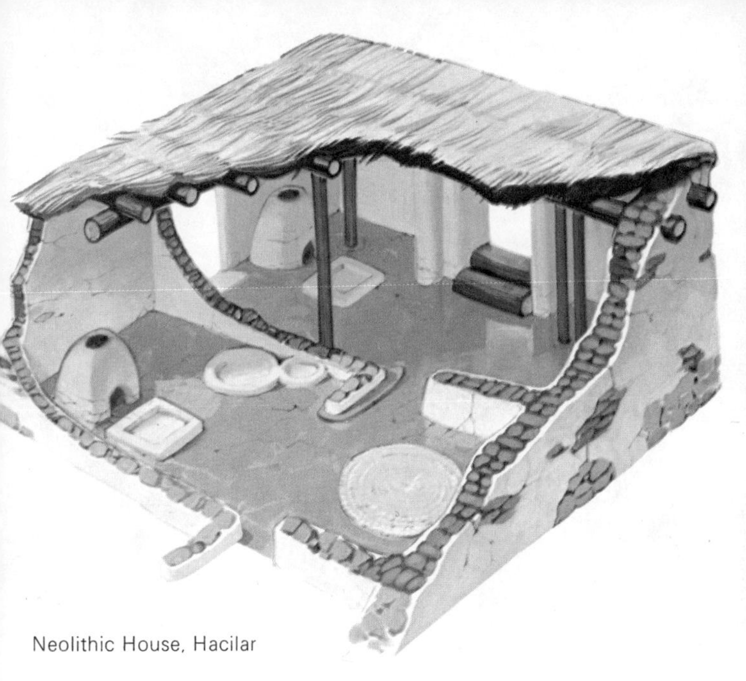
Neolithic House, Hacilar

over Jericho and enlarged it. In Asia Minor, and in Iraq there were, about 7000 B.C. similar pre-pottery Neolithic cultures. Around 6000 B.C. pre-pottery Neolithic folk had sailed successfully to Cyprus and settled there. And by 6500 B.C. pottery was being made in Asia Minor and elsewhere. Pottery then appears in Iran, Syria and at Jarmo in Iraq a little before 6000 B.C.

Perhaps the most astonishing evidence of the progress made by Neolithic man was the development of Catal (pronounced 'Chatal') Hüyük in south-east Asia Minor. This town, begun about 6500 B.C. lasted almost a thousand years, but there were many re-buildings, as can be expected with mud-brick buildings. The houses of this city, which lay near an active volcano, were neatly planned and remarkably standardized. The people of Catal Hüyük were cattle keepers and agriculturalists who sowed a great variety of wheats. They had elaborate sanctuary buildings with complex rituals and an impressive accompanying art. Perhaps more cities will be discovered in the Middle East and in Europe as well.

Township, Khirokitia, Cyprus

The Neolithic in the Near East spreads

Around 5500 B.C. a Neolithic way of life ranged from Iran to the mainland of Greece. Already there is such a variety of cultures that it is impossible to trace influences. Everywhere there seems to be growth and expansion. There is evidence of trade and movements and there must have been an expansion of peoples looking for further fields and pastures.

Towns like Hacilar (from before 6000 B.C.) some 200 miles west of Catal Hüyük. were more ambitious and there is an occasional copper object. Marbles and similar game kit were found and most art objects excavated show great sophistication – while Northern Europe was still at a food-gathering, Mesolithic stage. Hacilar was deserted by 5000 B.C. Asia Minor will doubtless furnish other sites of this kind.

Since Babylonia, the land between the Euphrates and the Tigris, was to be the seed-bed of the first civilizations, it will be worth sketching, however briefly, some of the Neolithic cultures of those parts. Some culture features had spread very widely. For example, pottery of the Halaf type (about

5000 B.C.) can be found from Syria to Iran. The Halaf culture, which showed glimmerings of the use of copper and all the traits of a prosperous way of life, was displaced by invaders of the 'Ubaid culture before 4300 B.C.

The 'Ubaid culture developed strongly in Mesopotamia and it was at this time that cast bronze axes were made. But most important was the development of social and economic organization which had as its obvious product the gigantic mud-brick temples of Eridu or Tepe Gawra. Organization of religion, agriculture and trade needs records. By 3500 B.C. there were clay tablets with writing on them. It is not surprising that the words and topics refer to gods, kings, weights, sheep. There were over thirty signs for different kinds of sheep almost at the beginning of writing.

The 'Uruk' period (3500–2900 B.C.) followed, a time when numerous cities came into being. In the Uruk period arose the civilizations of Sumeria.

The word 'Neolithic' has been in use just over a hundred years; it is becoming clear that in the next ten years we shall learn more than we did in the last hundred.

Jericho man reconstructed from a plastered Jericho skull.

Neolithic: Africa and Asia

The first Neolithic settlers in Africa appeared in the Nile valley and in parts of Libya; this was probably between 5000–4500 B.C. The sites that have been discovered, for example, in the Fayum, and later ones in the Sudan, show evidence of a variety of cultures with skilled flint industries, good pottery, cattle herding and agriculture. The spread after that was slower because of physical barriers. In parts of Africa below the Equator there was no Neolithic proper and only a late, gradual transfer from 'Middle Stone Age' cultures to 'Late Stone Age' cultures with stockholding, some agriculture. This was often the state of affairs until iron came.

But there were some notable diffusions of Neolithic ways to certain parts of Africa. Examples might include arrivals in West Africa, notably the Cape Verde area, the Congo and equatorial forest areas (Tumban culture). The forest environments of this kind have not unexpectedly furnished evidence of polished stone axes for forest clearance. Other examples of African Neolithic cultures are the Gumban and Njoroan of East Africa. These well-equipped pastoral cultures of Kenya and neighbouring areas used a variety of well-made artefacts such as polished axes, pestles and mortars. Unfortunately dating is difficult and the time-range can only be put tentatively as 3000–500 B.C. Some of these cultures eventually received or made iron goods without going through a copper or bronze age.

Neolithic stone implements, China

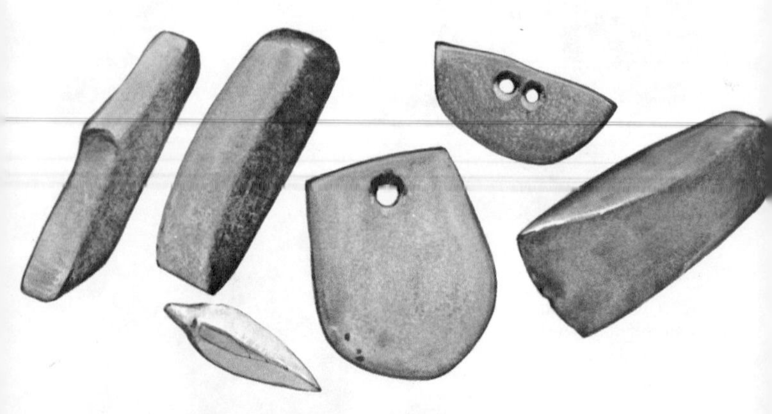

Chinese Neolithic pots

The Neolithic of the Indian sub-continent is thought to have its roots in Afghanistan, Baluchistan and Sind. Connections with Iran and Mesopotamia are being continually discussed but evidence for links is still tenuous. There has recently been little reason for doubting that in northern Afghanistan a pottery Neolithic culture of some sort was in existence as early as 5300 B.C. By 2600 B.C. or thereabouts farming and stockbreeding was well established in the Indus valley. It was in this valley that there arose a great civilization with great cities and its own system of writing. One of these cities was more than a mile across. Most readers have heard of Harappa in the Punjab and Mohenjo-daro in Sind, both in Pakistan. This civilization, as impressive for its planning and organization as for its plumbing, is not yet completely dated, but a peak period of about 2300–1750 A.D. has been suggested.

The Neolithic of southern Siberia is in some ways analogous to that of Iran and nearby areas where cultures like the

Mesolithic developed settled ways of life around 5000 B.C. At sites like Jeitun in Turkmenia, near the Iran border, one may find blades, microliths, bone sickles with flint teeth and a gaily painted pottery. The Siberian Neolithic of the Baikal area dates from about 3000 B.C. onwards. It had bone points of seemingly 'Upper Palaeolithic' type together with a distinctive pottery, some of it possessing impressions of nets pressed against it. The later Siberian cultures of the Lena area are thought to be ancestral, if only collaterally ancestral, to certain early pottery-using cultures of Canada and the United States, which seems to have come into existence independently of the Central American pottery makers.

The Neolithic in China may have arisen among Mesolithic peoples in the north of the country as early as 5000 B.C. At the moment it is possible here to point out only the main

Bath building and pottery from Mohenjo-daro

Art from Afghanistan and the Indus Valley.

groups. Some of the earliest finds of items made or used by Neolithic folk are from the Ordos desert of Inner Mongolia, and in Manchuria. Possibly better dated is the Yangshao of the Yellow River area which is thought to begin about 3000 B.C. Yangshao pottery is skilfully made and shows traces of turning. The patterns on these pots are lively. By the time that the Lung-shan culture of about 2000 B.C. was established we find a thin-walled black pottery which shows possible evidence of the use of the wheel. At about this time there may have been emigration into Malaysia and the Pacific.

In Japan the full story of the Neolithic has not yet been worked out but the pottery Neolithic of the Jomōn period appears to begin very early, perhaps before 4000 B.C.

New World cultures

America's prehistory is in some respects very different from that of the Old World. It is often easier to refer to it as the 'Pre-Columbian' period, since it is the coming of Columbus that marks the end of America's prehistory.

After 2000 B.C. in southern and middle America we find evidence of villages and what goes under the name of 'ceremonial centres'. The earliest of these centres appear to have been in Peru but the really striking ones were in

Mexico, where after 1000 B.C. impressive circular, stepped mounds acted as centres for highly organized communities. One of the better known of these was the Olmec ceremonial site (*c.* 1000–400 B.C.) to be found at La Venta on an island in Tabasco, Mexico.

At about the same time temple centres, often of ambitious stonework, were established in Peru. Cotton was cultivated there before 1000 B.C. and the later textiles of the South Americans before Columbus have been some of the finest weaves ever made by man.

While it is possible to discuss the story of the cultures of Peru and Mexico as distinct units, the ancient peoples of what are now the United States are difficult to isolate or classify. The distinctive pottery of the so-called 'Woodland' cultures has a date range spreading from nearly 1000 B.C.

Llama, Alpaca, Vicuna, South American animals.

Many of our food plants originate from America.

to A.D. 800. One may note here their huge mounds (either for rituals and for burials) and their elegant stone tobacco pipes. Not all the 'Woodland' peoples were agriculturalists since some were Arctic hunters.

Another group of traditions may be exemplified by the Mogollon (roughly 100 B.C. to A.D. 1500), the Hohokam (roughly 100 B.C.–A.D. 1400) and the Anazazi (after 100 B.C.–A.D. 1700). These were centred on Arizona, New Mexico and Colorado.

The Mogollon were well organized in their agriculture and in their villages and had well-designed houses. The Anazazi culture has become familiar because of its skills in basket-making and for the complex villages (pueblos) in which they lived. The desert-based Hohokam (who had links with Mexico) produced pots as gay and varied as the best in Old World cultures.

American archaeology offers some useful parallels for European workers.

Fall of the Pre-Columbians

In Middle America the culture that produced the great ceremonial centres such as La Venta and Monte Alban in Oaxaca, Mexico, and the gigantic sculptures of the period 1200–600 B.C. has been labelled 'Olmec'. This was one tradition among several of a priestly or theocratic world that persisted until the coming of the Spaniards. In the Yucatan peninsula of Mexico there arose the Maya, a civilization which had its first stages as early as 600 B.C. though the classic period was between about A.D. 250 and 900. It was a culture that depended spiritually not merely on the gods but on the fertility of maize. Their picture writing largely eludes us but their calendar system has been understood enough to show us that in some ways it was more accurate than anything the Romans or the Greeks could achieve.

In Mexico also there arose the culture represented by the huge city of Teotihuacan, a great pilgrimage and market centre. The Teotihuacan civilization lasted from about 300 B.C. to about A.D. 600 when the city was destroyed.

As elsewhere these civilizations were eclipsed or destroyed by 'barbarians'. Warriors largely displaced priestly rulers. Thus it was that the Toltecs and the Mixtecs ruled the roost in Mexico until a small group was allowed a toehold in the Valley of Mexico. This group, a group of perhaps only a thousand originally, was known as the Aztecs. Gathering strength in the 12th century A.D. these peoples (who shared both the organizational skills and the power-hunger of the Romans and the Normans) established a great empire which in the 16th century was defeated, ironically by a rather small group of Spaniards.

In South America a minor kingdom of the Andes that flourished just before A.D. 1000 began to consolidate and a smaller group, the Incas, which had begun to expand around A.D. 1200 staged an aggressive expansion in the 15th century. They had just settled their dynastic squabbles when Francesco Pizarro in 1532–33 won the whole empire with a handful of men.

Items made in a 2000-year period before Columbus

Neolithic pots from the Danube basin

Neolithic cultures enter Europe

Well before 5000 B.C. the first farmers had established themselves in northern Greece. In the next thousand years the Neolithic way of life spread as far as the Low Countries. It took another thousand years in order to complete the spread of the New Stone Age to the British Isles, Scandinavia and the West of Europe.

The first arrivals seem to have brought with them much that reminds us of their near eastern origins: some used mud bricks and others had inscribed objects of eastern origins. But as these farmers and pastoralists spread up the river valley of south-eastern Europe, and especially the Danube area, there were developed pottery and other features which were genuinely European. Some groups were probably more mobile than others and may have moved on because they had exhausted the soil, others stayed put. The site of Karanovo in Bulgaria was occupied for over 3000 years and the 'tell' or heap of successive deposits is over 12 metres high.

In the fifth millennium B.C. occurred one important group called the 'Linear' pottery culture because of the distinctive pottery. However they deserve our attention for the long rectangular houses (some over 30 metres long) clustered into 'villages'. In the meanwhile Neolithic cultures had been established in southern Italy and eastern Spain, but the main pattern which finally crystallized out in Europe between 4000 and 2500 B.C. resolved itself into (1) a 'Western' group including among others the Chassey-Cortaillod cultures of France and Switzerland and the wares of the western Mediterranean which were decorated with shell-edge impressions (impressed ware) and the British Early Neolithic cultures; (2) the Danish and North German areas with the strange 'Funnel Beakers' and (3) the Boian (Romania) and Tripolye (Ukraine) cultures.

Trade of some sort was promoted throughout the Neolithic, at first in shells and stone and possibly salt, and later on, but before 2500 B.C. copper from the Carpathians and elsewhere was being traded and used.

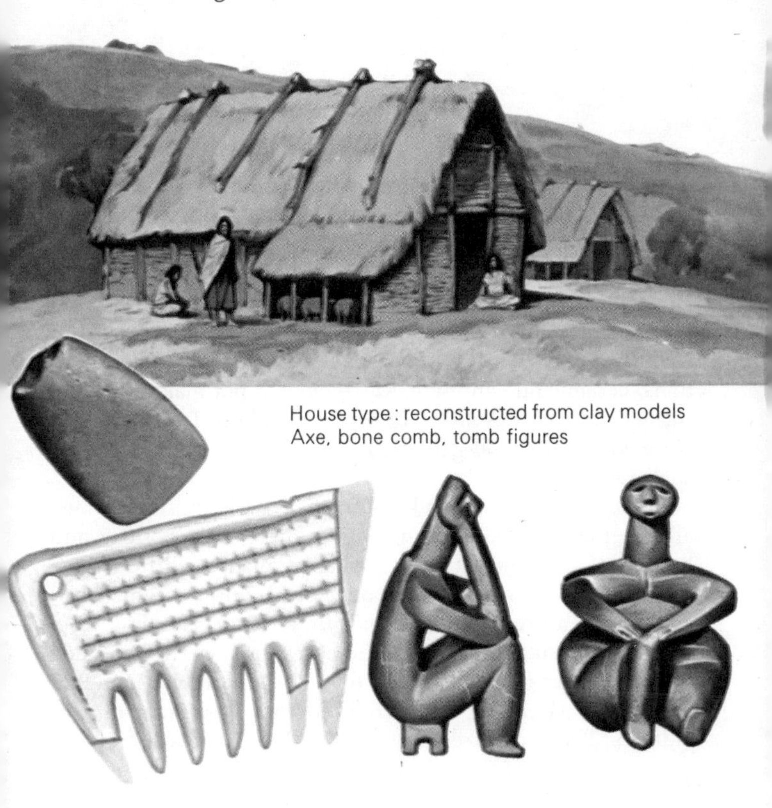

House type: reconstructed from clay models
Axe, bone comb, tomb figures

The Neolithic in Northern Europe

In Poland and Germany the first Neolithic arrivals were well established between 5000 and 4000 B.C. Their origins can be found in the earlier Danubian Neolithic. In the Schleswig-Holstein area, which lies between Denmark and Germany, the Ellerbek culture (4500–4000 B.C.) has ample marks of a Neolithic way of life: wood spades, pots with conical bottoms, ceramic oil lamps etc. Knowledge of pot-making seeped through to the Mesolithic Ertebølle people in Denmark who were generally food-gatherers, depositing vast middens of shell remains.

In the Rhineland we find around 4000 B.C. a culture, named after a place called Rossen, with a distinctive pottery and houses of an unusual trapeze-shaped plan. A little to the north of this area there then developed cultures which had common features to be found in a band running from Holland to Poland. Among these features is the so-called Funnel Beaker (Trichterbecher or 'TRB') of around 3500 B.C. Saxony in Germany has produced many remains of this culture. These cultures are not the direct ancestors of our

British Neolithic. A further mingling of cultures took place before the mix was ready for emigrations to Britain.

Switzerland and Northern France both received a full Neolithic before 3500 B.C., in Northern France there is a transition from pick-using cultures, such as the Campignian, which merges uncertainly into such groups as the Chassey culture. Many early Neolithic cultures in France contain geometric microliths harking back to the Mesolithic.

Of great importance in the development of a northern Neolithic is the development in North Germany, the Netherlands and southern Sweden, of 'Passage Graves'. These huge stone burial structures (generally after 3000 B.C.) are also found in France, Britain, Spain and part of the north coasts of the Western Mediterranean. But there are distinctive local features in the northern zone, though the basic type is still a circular or many-angled burial chamber with an approach passage serving some ritual or social requirement.

After this the Neolithic in the North becomes more and more complex and varied pots and burial customs pose enormous problems for prehistorians.

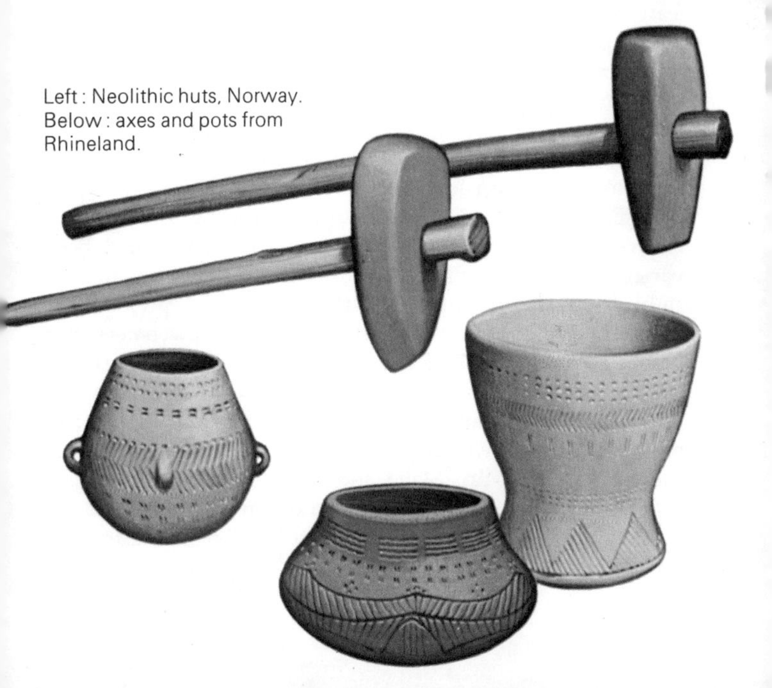

Left: Neolithic huts, Norway.
Below: axes and pots from Rhineland.

The Neolithic in some Mediterranean Lands

Like most human occurrences, the entry of the first farmers and pastoralists into southern Europe was an untidy process. Though some of the earliest arrivals were in the Danube area and Greece, we find no simple fanning out from bridgeheads. Irregular, sporadic arrivals at separate spots seem to have been the method employed, though this may be only the picture coming from the chances of discovery. In Italy, for example, the new settlers seem to have chosen Liguria and parts of Italy's deep south, and this not long after 5000 B.C. Sicily and Malta were not far behind in receiving independent settlers. We have to gain more knowledge, though, before we can say what sorts of boats were used and how they selected new areas in which they were going to settle.

France, after the artistic glories of its Upper Palaeolithic, may have become a backwater of Mesolithic cultures for a long time. The first clearly defined makers of pots were on the scene around 4500–4000 B.C.

The details of the arrival of the Neolithic in Greece are still being sorted out and there have been many unexpected features. In Thessaly remains of the equipment and daily doings of a *pre-pottery* Neolithic have been found and attested. This can go back to before 6000 B.C. Enough features have been found to enable one to see ultimate links with the way of life in, say, Cyprus or ancient Jericho. At that time prospectors for obsidian (for tools) were ranging through some of the Greek isles.

In many ways Spain and Portugal offer most of the current inducements to students of the Neolithic. There had been varied, strong Mesolithic cultures in this great peninsula right from the beginning of the post-glacial period. The mingling which occurred with Neolithic newcomers just before 4000 B.C. enabled the original inhabitants to maintain some of their old ways. For example, the rock paintings which are descendants of the ancient art of the Palaeolithic now appear to show animals led by cords. Perhaps it was in these times in Spain, Malta and elsewhere, that those who organized the burying of their dead began to evolve attitudes and techniques which later came to fruition in the form of burials beneath stones.

Neolithic objects from Spain with conjectural reconstruction of mixed farming and hunting activities.

Reconstructions of causewayed camps could be misleading

The first farmers in Britain

Some time before 3500 B.C. the first Neolithic settlers came to the British Isles. Where they came from is difficult to say but evidence from related pottery found abroad has been thought to show links with France, the Low Countries and even Germany. Among the earlier settlements, around 3500 B.C. dated by radio-carbon are Windmill Hill in Wiltshire, Hembury in Devon, and in Ireland, as at Dalkey Island, County Dublin and elsewhere.

One school of thought argued very plausibly that Mesolithic food gatherers gradually learned the Neolithic way of life from the newcomers and gradually became Neolithic (or 'Secondary Neolithic'). However the highly pitted decorations of the Secondary Neolithic pots are very different from the generally plain Windmill Hill pots. Some argued that the Early British Neolithic (such as at Windmill Hill), and the 'Secondary' wares found in the Thames and in the East

Midlands were parallel developments of broadly the same cultures as the Windmill Hill 'Western' group.

One of the better known features of the early Neolithic of Britain are the 'causewayed camps' which are concentric enclosures, some of them hundreds of feet in diameter. The rings of ditches are broken by 'causeways'. Some have suggested that they are 'ritual' sites, and others that they are 'tribal centres', periodic meeting places for exchange of goods, and for ceremonies. Among the better-known examples of causewayed camps are Windmill Hill and Hembury. There were two near London Airport. These structures are similar to causewayed camps in the early French Neolithic.

The first Neolithic settlers had varied funerary practices. Some burials, perhaps of chiefs, were twofold. First the corpse might have a spell in a mortuary enclosure, then it would go into a long barrow of earth. At about the same time burials were introduced which used great stone slabs (megaliths) for structures known as 'chamber tombs'.

Neolithic items from Britain

Later Neolithic Britain

Almost entirely a British phenomenon (there are some continental parallels) are the 'ritual' sites called henges. Basically they are circular ditches with one or more entrances; the sizes vary. Many of them show evidence of an internal ring of pits which were sometimes the sockets for uprights of timber or stone. They range across the later Neolithic of England and Scotland, a period roughly between 2100 and 1600 B.C. Some famous henges are of the Beaker period at the end of the Neolithic. In North Britain there are many stone circles which are still little understood and even more mysterious are the so-called processional ways or 'cursuses' such as are found in Wiltshire and on the Continent.

The famous 'temple' of Stonehenge was started at the end of the Neolithic, about 1800 B.C. It was not the impressive

Avebury

monument the remains of which we see today. The site was then a circular area surrounded with a ditch and an inner bank made from its spoil. There was a ring of fifty-six 'ritual' holes ringing the inside. The next stage of Stonehenge was in the Beaker period.

Avebury also in Wiltshire, has been called a 'henge', though this huge structure – over 400 metres across – has many unusual features which include a great ditch and an avenue marked by stone uprights. A ritual centre of this kind will have had a complex history and one should not regard the whole monument as being built at one time. Most of the evidence points to the place being constructed in the main around 2000 B.C. or a century or two later.

The end of the Neolithic is, theoretically, marked by the first arrival of copper with the Beaker people.

The earliest Stonehenge, c. 1800 BC.

Megaliths

For European prehistorians megalithic (Greek *megas*, great, and *lithos* stone) chambered tombs have been an obvious feature of Western Europe, from Spain to Scandinavia and from the Orkneys to Sardinia and Apuglia. They range from the early Neolithic to the end of the Bronze Age. Such burials are not peculiar to Europe or the Neolithic. Megaliths and stone cists have been used in India's Iron Age, on Easter Island, in nineteenth-century Africa and in many other places. This is not evidence of inter-connected cultures or movements but simply of availability of stone and man's almost universal desire at one time or another to build seemly houses for his dead. In any case there is so much variety in megaliths – from the cist tombs of Bronze Age Japan to the Hunebedden of the Netherlands and from Maes Howe in Orkney to the Cueva de Menga in Spain – that it is impossible to generalize about their general structure, dating or ritual. Some megalithic tombs were used for a thousand years.

Other tombs have been looted or altered and many megaliths have been re-used over the years.

One British group is the 'gallery graves' from the west of Britain which is a *gallery* or chamber of stone slabs, sometimes with side compartments. A mound of earth or stones covered the whole. The West Kennet long barrow in Wiltshire is a typical example. The other group is the 'passage grave' of which Maes Howe, Orkney, is a fine example.

The archaeologist excavating chamber tombs has to be vigilant in looking for evidence of rituals (fires, food, broken items) at the entrance; he has to distinguish the successive heapings of bones or bodies taken from mortuary houses.

Left, New Grange, Ireland; view from the air.
Below, a carving at the entrance and, right, the interior

Prehistoric burials

Man's way of burying his dead in the Neolithic varied from land to land. Already in the Mesolithic funerary practices varied from burials in containers to the specialized collective burials of skulls. Burials ranged from casual dumping to interments of great complexity. In Britain a skeleton scattered through the ditch of a Neolithic causewayed camp might indicate indifference or violence. In Neolithic Japan a flexed body is buried in a shell midden. A touch of ceremony or sentiment is added by the placing at the head a jar containing an infant's bones.

Sometimes a burial is 'secondary': the body has been re-buried some time after death and after considerable decay has gone on. This has been noted in many Neolithic cultures from Britain (in megaliths) to the earlier Jericho.

Cremations have often been regarded as being introduced in the Bronze Age, but there are many Neolithic examples, such as in Greece where bodies were partially burned before burial not long after 5000 B.C. In Poland cremations of just

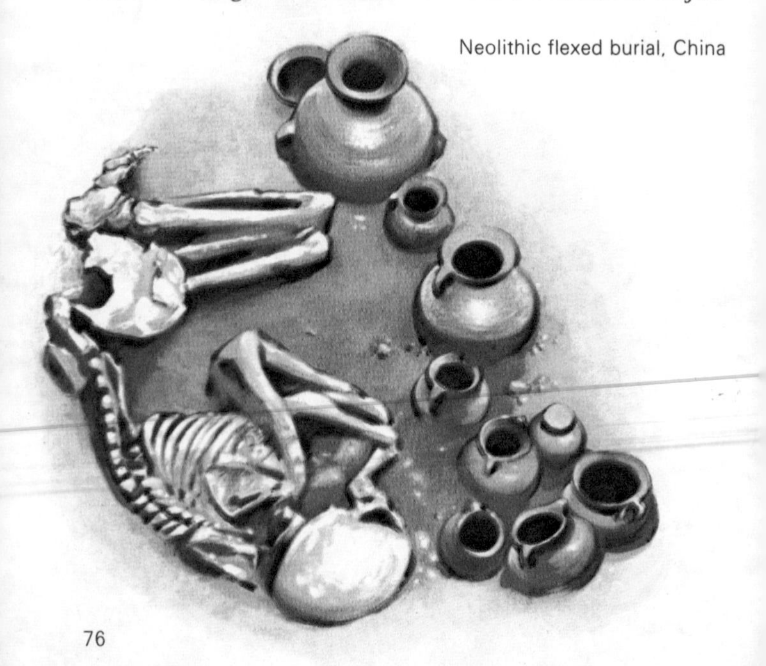

Neolithic flexed burial, China

Remains of a cremation, Iron Age, Finland

after 4000 B.C. were noted and in the late Neolithic of Czechoslovakia cremations were side by side with unburnt burials. In Germany cremations were found under Neolithic houses. Cremation was practiced in both halves of the American continent over 2000 years ago, and there are isolated examples of a late Stone Age site in Kenya (about 1000 B.C.) where elaborate cremation rites went on.

Throughout his researches the archaeologist must try to understand the mixed motives behind burials: placation of the dead; getting the help of the dead; helping the dead on their journey and equipping them for the after-life. He must learn to distinguish between continuing traditions and the custom of later peoples putting their dead in a megalith or barrow of a thousand years before.

A burial must not be studied merely for its jewellery, crockery and ritual paraphernalia: burials and, more especially, family groups and cemeteries can teach the researcher much about disease, growth, nutrition and heredity.

Man and metals: Copper

Copper ores are sometimes blue or green, so once the art of smelting copper was discovered it was easy for prospectors to seek out more ores. Iron or tin have less obvious ores and they are more difficult to work.

While copper is not a hard metal it is possible to make more efficient tool edges with it than with stone. While generally the earliest copper tools were cast in the Near East after 6000 B.C. there are occasional examples of cast of forged items earlier than that.

Man swiftly learned to use the metal efficiently and economically. A central midrib in a slim dagger increased strength but cut out unnecessary use of expensive metal. Arrowheads could quickly be given sharp barbs and tools such as saws become more practical when metal, instead of flint or stone, is available.

Since copper was not instantly adopted most cultures went through a stage when stone tools were used side by side with those of copper. The term *chalcolithic* has been used to denote this stage. Thus at Hacilar and Catal Hüyük in Asia Minor

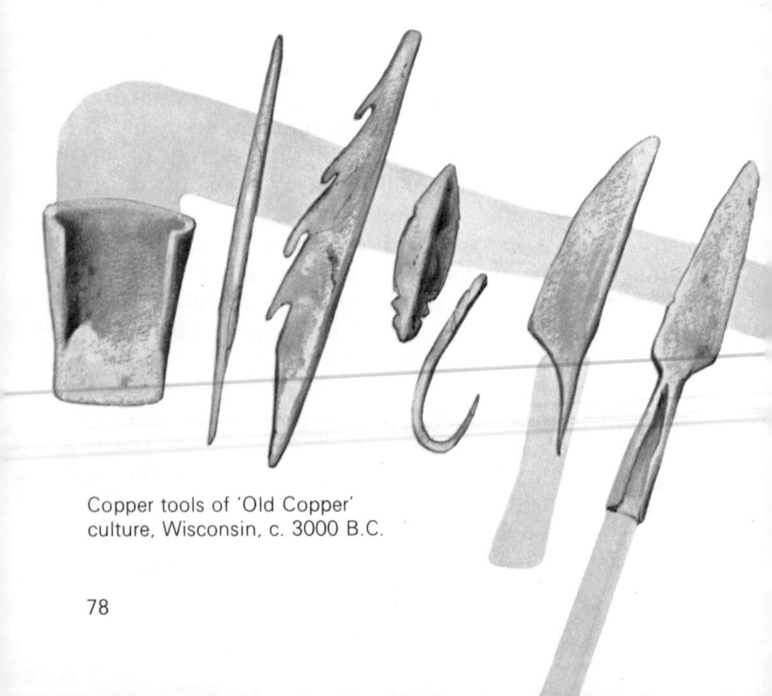

Copper tools of 'Old Copper' culture, Wisconsin, c. 3000 B.C.

there was some copper in use, mainly for ornaments, around 5500 B.C. and in some cases a thousand years earlier. Perhaps this was hardly a true chalcolithic period, but at Siyalk in Iran, and at Uruk in Iraq, copper implements were in use at the same time as stone ones a little before 3500 B.C. In Britain, at the end of the third millennium B.C. the Beaker Folk had metal daggers but they also put traditional flint daggers and arrowheads into their burials. In the Deccan, India, in the middle of the second millennium B.C. people used blade tools of flint-like chert but they also had elegant fish hooks of copper and cast shaft-axes.

It should not be forgotten that man learned to use copper in the New World, though in a different way. For example, in Wisconsin the 'Old Copper' Indians made knives, awls, barbed harpoons, and fish-hooks of copper not long after 3000 B.C. But they did not smelt the copper. Instead they mined 'native copper' which was found, without needing smelting, in volcanic and other rocks. This copper was hammered or, perhaps, heated and hammered. The Incas too, worked in copper and indeed in gold, silver, tin and lead.

Copper ore (malachite) axe casting in a stone mould

Bronze working

Archaeologists in the past made too sharp a distinction between the Stone Age and the Bronze Age. Copper was used first and existed side by side with surviving stone tool types. Even when bronze (an alloy of copper and tin) came in, flint arrowheads and scrapers still went on being used. The period 3000–2000 B.C. was the time when bronze came to be widely used in the Old World. In America, some copper and bronze working was devised before the appearance of the Europeans. In Colombia, in South America, a gold and copper alloy was worked.

Bronze was generally cast in moulds of clay, stone or other materials. Elaborate casting was done by making a wax or wood model and embedding it in clay. Metal poured into the mould with the wax model melted out the wax which left the shape in the clay mould. Bronze in the Bronze Age of the Old World was sometimes cold-worked by hammering. Lead was used as an additive in both Europe and Egypt, possibly to help flow into the mould.

Bronze reached the extremes of the Old World roughly at about the same time; in Britain around 1800 B.C. and China around 1500 B.C. The Chinese had already used copper for almost a thousand years.

Bronze was never cheap since the copper and the tin of the alloy had to come from different places. Scrap bronze was therefore a valuable commodity and one still hears about new finds of 'hoards' left by itinerant bronze-smiths. Such hoards contain an extraordinary variety of objects ranging from trumpet mouthpieces to cattle bells. They offer a useful cross-dating for objects.

It is ironical to find that in Europe, Asia and Africa some of the finest bronze work – such as hammered plate shields or cauldrons – is of the Iron Age. This is often what happens: when a material is eclipsed: its technologists reach high peaks of craftsmanship and technique. Bronze often survives in the soil much better than iron, so it might be possible for us to obtain a rather misleading picture about the extent to which it was used.

Bronze hoard from Leicestershire, of about the 7th century B.C.

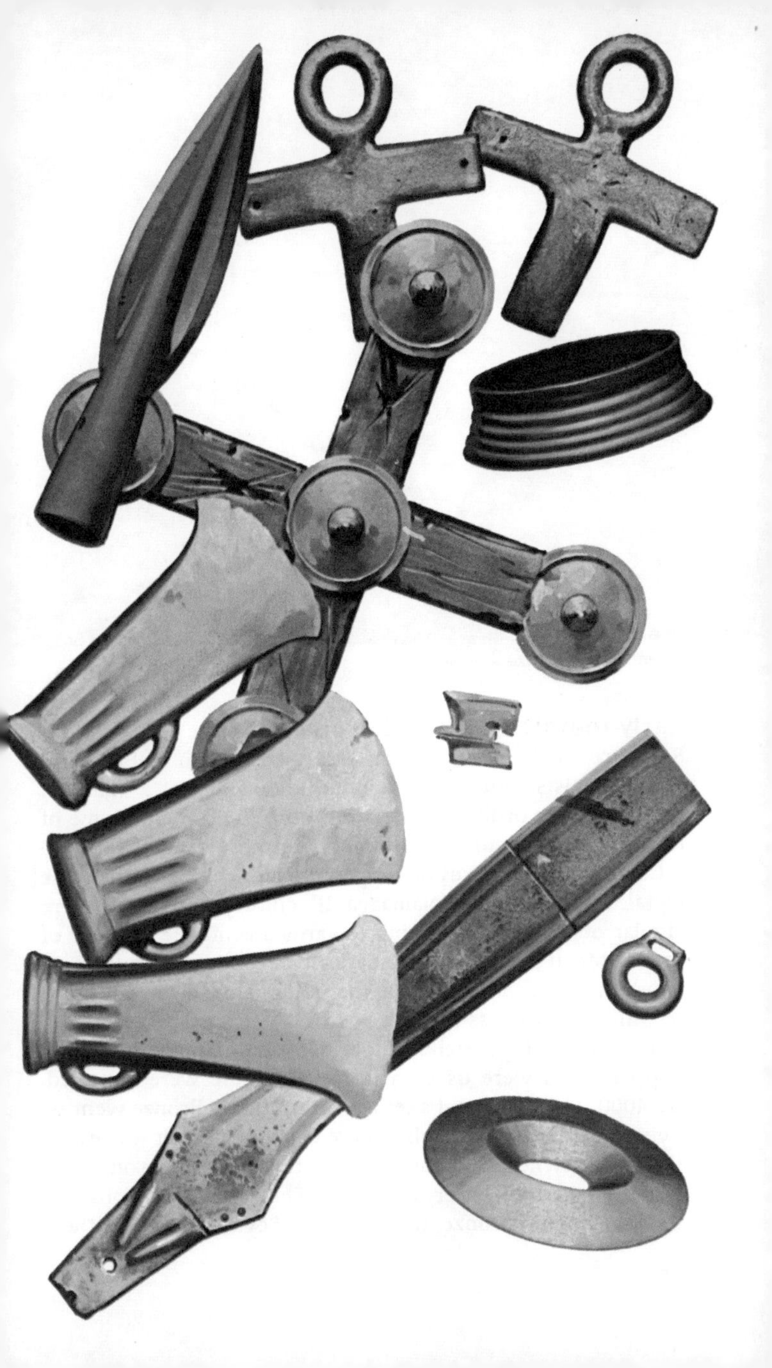

Ingots from Bronze Age wreck

Early metal: Asia and Europe

Southern Turkestan is not an area well known to European archaeologists, but a considerable knowledge of a complex Neolithic way of life is emanating from the U.S.S.R. Some of these Neolithic cultures (roughly between 5300 and 4300 B.C.) already used axes of copper and spearheads of the same metal. This was the 'Namazga II' culture and there were similar ones in Asia working towards a complete mastery of metal. Metal does not automatically change one culture to another, but in metal we see the potentiality of not so much technical progress as of power-getting and warfare.

In Iran, at Tepe Sialk, before 4500 B.C. hammered native copper items were used; a little later these were annealed. By 4000 B.C. cast metal axes are found there. Bronze went on being used in Asia and elsewhere even when iron was established elsewhere. Examples are the elegant bronzes of Luristan, in Iran (after 900 B.C.). The varied weapons and implements of bronze used by the Scythians in Southern

Russia around the 7th century B.C. have shapes like those already being made in iron in Europe.

Copper and bronze may have entered Europe as 'personal imports' or as trade from centres in Europe controlled or initiated by traders or prospectors from the eastern Mediterranean. But a proper bronze age needs craftsmen and smiths. What persuaded them to move into Europe? Perhaps the home bases in the Near East were being shaken at that time (just before 2000 B.C.) by internal unrest or barbarian attacks. Whatever the reason smiths, craftsmen and eventually bronze scrap-merchants were soon established in Europe.

There is no doubt that trade became an important element of Bronze Age life, but details have often to be inferred. Only rarely have wrecks been found like that off Cape Gelidonya, in Turkey. This little ship, sunk around 1200 B.C. not only had a varied load of ingots and other goods, but also a set of 'international' weights for handling business in many countries. By then trade extended from the Baltic areas and Britain through much of Europe to the Mediterranean.

Amber and gold beads from various parts of Europe. Scandinavian boat types.

Hittite gate
Mycenaean dagger
Cretan figure

Cultures and civilizations of the Mediterranean

By 2000 B.C. several of the great civilizations were well established. Egypt was beginning its twelfth dynasty and the first great dynasty of Babylon which was to reach its zenith in the reign of Hammurabi (1792–1750 B.C.). In Crete the 'Middle Minoan' period produced buildings so bold in their concept and organization that the word 'palace' has to be used in describing the residences of this civilization which was based on large-scale, efficient trading. The dating and culture of the Minoans are being reconsidered.

The Bronze Age of Greece, generally known as the Helladic period, was pre-Greek but already the national skill in pottery and sculpture was being foreshadowed. It is assumed that Greek speakers were on the scene around 1900 B.C. How far the Minoan civilization of Crete was related to the Helladic of Greece has still to be sorted out. By 1500 B.C. there was rising the Mycenaean civilization with its palaces or fortresses at Mycenae, Tiryns and Pylos. Cretan power seems to have diminished to nothing by 1400 B.C. and the Mycenaeans then lorded it over the Mediterranean as rulers and as traders. As early as 1400 B.C. a system of writing was in use, a script deciphered as being Greek only as recently as in the 1950s. The Mycenaean world is largely that of Homeric poems, though they were put into the form we know in the Iron Age. Troy really existed; indeed there were several Troys, and it is possibly around 1350–1250 B.C. that the Homeric one fell.

About 1200 B.C. there were great disturbances in the east and west of the ancient world. Great empires such as that of the Hittites of Asia Minor came to nought at that time. Mycenaean power lasted a little longer but by 1050 or 1000 B.C. Mycenaean glory was preserved only in epic poetry and in surviving ruins. Greece, and later, western Asia Minor were nevertheless a continuation and development of the culture of the Mycenaeans. The great expansion of the Greeks, whose colonies stretched from the Black Sea to Spain was in the 8th, 7th and 6th centuries B.C. The great 'classical' period was the 5th century B.C.

Reconstruction of Mycenaean equipment and jewellery

Cheek-piece, Luristan

Barbarian bronze in Europe and Asia

It will take some time before early metal finds are re-examined to see if they are of copper or bronze. But it is probable that in Mesopotamia bronze was being used occasionally around 3000 B.C. In Iran or the Caspian area bronze was being used very early in the third millennium. We should note here that these first users of metal were chalcolithic, that is they used both metal and stone implements. In India chalcolithic cultures were as early as 2500 B.C. but true bronze was much later. China was using copper at about the same time but the first significant bronzes are of the Shang dynasty (post 1500 B.C.)

Metal, both copper and bronze was in use in Greece as early as 2400 B.C. It has been said by some scholars that the word *Cyprus* means 'copper'.

Perhaps the chief features to be noticed about the Bronze Age of Europe is the quantity of trade by land and sea. A dagger like that of a 'Mycenaean' type from Greece has been found in Cornwall. On Stonehenge itself are carvings of daggers that can be said to have an Aegean ancestry. The wealthy Wessex culture has items in it that also occur in the Únetice culture of Czechoslovakia. Amber, from the shores of the Baltic, has been found in Greece and Wessex with similar gold decorations.

The horse is thought to have been domesticated in the steppes before 2000 B.C. Very often the domestication of the horse can only be inferred from metal finds such as parts of bridles, cheek pieces, bits etc. Some antler cheek pieces have been noted in Britain. The date range of such items is around 2000–1500 B.C. Other species like the onager (a sort of ass) and the ox may have been persuaded quite early to pull carts. There are four-wheeled vehicles illustrated in pictographs drawn in Mesopotamia before 3000 B.C. In Holland, before 2000 B.C. four-wheel wagons trundled over log roads. There is ample evidence, even from the Neolithic, of vehicles shown in models or drawings. Little however is known about the origin of the wheel. It seems to have been the result of a deliberate design, not a gradual development.

Horse-breaking, Scythia. Lausitz pots

Urnfield areas shown by lighter colour

Between 2500 and 2300 B.C. there moved westwards from areas behind the Volga various people which are loosely described by archaeologists as being of the *Kurgan* cultures. By 2000 B.C. traces of their influence could be found from Scandinavia to Italy and from eastern France to Asia Minor. Already they had learned of the techniques developed in the Near East for working bronze. The buried their dead in barrows (kurgans) and not only had distinctive axes of stone or metal but also sturdy wagons. The kurgan peoples, like some others, have been claimed as the first bearers of Indo-European speech into Europe.

The cultures that developed from or followed the kurgan makers were numerous. One can only mention here a few of the cultures that should be familiar to serious students of European prehistory. For example, one may mention the Unétice (or 'Aunjetitz') culture of around 1800–1450 B.C. with its savage weapon, the bronze halberd. This localized culture of Central Europe marks the first times when bronze was used on a large scale.

An example of cultures in Europe in the Middle Bronze Age is that of the so-called Tumulus cultures. They developed existing techniques of burying the dead in pits under mounds. Flourishing in areas west of the Unétice area, they reached their peak around 1500–1300 B.C.

Of great archaeological interest is the group known by the omnibus title of the Urnfield cultures with a massive time-range of 1400–700 B.C. Beginning in the Danube area, and subsequently spreading to central Europe and Italy, this culture (or rather a bunch of cultures) often buried their cremated dead in pits or urn graves which accumulated into large cemeteries. The cemetery of Lausitz in Silesia has lent its name (as 'Lausitz' or 'Lusatian') to aspects of this culture.

Bronze wheel, Switzerland. Bit, Germany. Urn, Britain

Beakers from Britain and Europe with copper and flint daggers

Beakers

At the end of the Neolithic period, when copper was coming into use in Europe, there appeared between 2500 and 1800 B.C. peoples who buried with their dead with tallish, decorated vessels called 'Beakers' by archaeologists. From Britain and Spain to Czechoslovakia and Hungary and as far south as Sicily these vessels were used and imitated. It has been noted that people as vigorous as the Romans and the Normans failed to establish themselves all over the British Isles yet the Beaker people or their influence did manage to do so. At least, the vessels spread far and wide; it is possible that we have here nothing more unusual than the distribution of the Cola bottle. We may thus be mistaken in speaking of the Beaker People; it is possible that we have just the travelling of a culture trait.

There is still considerable discussion as to the origin of the Beaker. Some have thought that the vessel type began its career in Spain and Portugal and that the vessel spread eastwards. It has also been argued that there were 'refluxes' which may have brought it back to the place of its birth.

Though most scholars would say that the Beakers of Britain came from the Low Countries there are suggestions that France and Spain may have also dispatched either the vessels and their users or the techniques of making and using them. Beaker varieties in Britain vary both in date and in area of distribution.

With Beakers go fine gold ornaments, skilfully made flint daggers and arrowheads as well as copper daggers. While in Mesopotamia and Egypt there were fully developed civilizations, Europe (apart from the Minoan world) was hardly at an advanced stage of culture. Yet in many ways the Beaker people came in as a sort of leaven. Things started to happen not long after their arrival. They produced a taste for complexity and expansion. The henges of Britain and much of the Stonehenge we know were built in Beaker times. It has even been suggested by serious scholars that Indo-European languages came in to Europe with the Beaker users.

The second Stonehenge, c. 1600 B.C.

Bronze Age Britain

Metalwork found in Britain that can be dated to before 2000 B.C., whether it is copper or bronze, can be said to have been an import. After that date, and especially after 1800 B.C., some metal objects were manufactured in the British Isles.

The plain, flat axes, the broad daggers, the long rapiers and dirks as well as the 'palstave' (a cast axe designed for a split, crook-head wood handle) and many dress accessories form obvious components of the first half of the British Bronze Age and most museums possess examples. It should not be forgotten that flint arrowheads and certain stone axe-hammers still went on being used while metal was expensive. But within a few centuries Britain and Ireland began to gain importance for producing bronze and gold objects. A complex typology of bronzework is today keeping many archaeologists busy as is assessing trade and craft relations between Britain and the continent.

The second half of the Bronze Age (in Britain it bumps into the Iron Age around 500 B.C.) produces socketed axes, leaf-

Bronze Age spearheads

shaped slashing swords and a great variety of spearheads. But weapons are not the only finds; there are trumpets, hammers, razors, chisels and, indeed, many unidentified objects to be found in the tinkers' hoards of Britain.

Variations in pottery are too numerous to be listed here, but one can mention a few examples of types that may be seen in many local museums. In parts of southern Britain around 1400–900 B.C. appears a distinctive series of so-called bucket or barrel urns, occasionally going with smaller 'globular' urns. Better known is the 'food vessel' of the period around 1700–1300 B.C. which is found patchily but frequently in all parts of Britain and Ireland. Collared urns (the top is really like a turned-down collar) also occur in many parts of Britain including Wessex with its wealthy culture of the period 1650–1400 B.C. In North Britain many urns of the Bronze Age are decorated swags of 'encrusted' ornaments for which Irish parallels have been found. Though it has been difficult to correlate pots and metalwork in Britain, it is easy to visualize great variations in activities and peoples.

Pots and tools of the British Bronze Age

Burial mounds

'Barrows', 'tumuli', 'Hügelgräber' are mounds, generally round, built over burials, especially of the Bronze Age. This is a simplification because there were round barrows in Europe and elsewhere in the Neolithic and in historic periods. One should not forget the 'long' barrows which are found in many parts of the world. Mounds of this kind went on being heaped for a long time: the Iron Age Hallstatt warriors of Central Europe still lie under barrows, as do Scythian leaders; American Indian chiefs more than a thousand years before Columbus had mounds of various shapes dumped over them. One may find barrows in Poland, Albania, Scotland or Japan.

It is impossible to make a general statement that explains why the influential men and women of the past felt their dignity and afterlife would be enhanced by a barrow. So esteemed were barrows that in Britain Romans, Saxons and others inserted their dead into Bronze Age barrows, pro-

Schematized 'bell' and 'disc' barrows

Top : mound, U.S.A. ; Bottom, barrows, U.S.S.R.

ducing many a problem for the excavator.

So fascinating are barrows that though there are thousands that have survived ploughing or erosion, few have not been mauled by plunderers or inept archaeologists.

The archaeologist who wishes to learn more about barrows soon discovers that they are not simple domes of earth heaped over a burial. Some have ditches round them while others are found to show evidence of a ring of stakes that once stood round it. This would not be unexpected, but some barrows, skilfully dissected by the archaeologist show a complex sequence of events. The corpse might be cremated and a little wooden house put over it for a time, then a stake circle was put round the area and after an interval soil was heaped over the collapsed hut. After several more stages (which may include additional burials) the barrow as we see it today was heaped up.

'Ritual' sites before and after the Bronze Age

Many jokes are made about archaeologists who are said to explain anything they can't understand or recognize as a 'ritual' object or site. Interpreting even a minor find can be fraught with problems. For example, a small hole in the ground containing burnt twigs may have been for a nearby burial – or it may have been a small fire for smoke-curing hides. Ritual behaviour, when excavated, is sometimes hard to interpret as such. However certain features such as sacrificial burials under structures and similar finds can occasionally help one make intelligent suggestions.

Many sites such as the 'henges' of Britain are thought to be of a ritual nature. These circular enclosures, often with timber uprights and occasionally with stone ones, range in time from the Neolithic to the Bronze Age. Often such places were used for centuries. Stonehenge in Wiltshire began as a

The final stage of Stonehenge, c. 1400 B.C.

timber structure and finally ended up as the impressive structure that has partially survived to this day. Though Stonehenge is one of the more impressive prehistoric sites in Europe, circular structures with superficially similar features have been found in other parts of Europe. A late Iron Age one, for example, has been found in Romania. The most astonishing claims have been made for both Stonehenge and this Romanian circle. They have been called 'computers' and so on. While it has been shown that some of these structures *may* have had astronomical connections, the reader is urged not to accept, without demanding a full explanation, the mathematical aspects of these structures – especially when the conclusions are derived with the spurious accuracy that comes from reading off angles from a drawing on a reduced scale. Fortunately many more scientifically trained workers are appearing on the scene and in the next decade we shall have a truer picture of the mathematical side of megalithic and other structures.

Europe and Asia: end of the Bronze Age

Words like Bronze Age and Iron Age, it must be repeated, do not carry automatic dating. It depends on what part of the world is being considered. Indeed archaeologists sometimes find it very annoying to be made to label an object or site sharply; so often there are overlaps of culture features. The Three Ages system has not always clarified prehistory.

In China for example the first bronze objects emerged, as a result of contacts with central Asia, sometimes around 1500 B.C. In Britain bronze had arrived some centuries earlier in a world with probably a less centralized social organization. In China we are in the Shang Dynasty and there are elaborate sites of politico-religious importance such as was found near Anyang in Honan, north China. The dating of much of this portion of China's story depends on records which are not highly trustworthy until after 1000 B.C. Chinese craftsmanship in working bronze lay not so much in the skilled making of weaponry as in the making of elaborate 'ritual' vessels. Such vessels went on being made for over a thousand years, and well after the time the Chinese had learnt to make cast iron (about 600–400 B.C.). The rest of the world went on using wrought iron until recent times. Often an invention is made before the economic and cultural climate is ready for it.

Moving back to the west to, for example, Greece, we should try to consider what the Late Bronze Age meant in that area. Oddly enough some of the people who, around 1300–1000 B.C. shattered the Bronze Age *status quo* in areas in and around what we now call Greece, were Greeks themselves. It is very hard to sort out which people and what circumstances brought down the Minoan and Mycenaean cultures. The Greeks themselves knew that they were descendants of different groups of incoming Greeks (e.g. the Dorians, Ionians etc.) who came at different times. So even if the Mycenaean civilization was Greek as the Linear B tablets indicate, there is no reason why the Bronze Age world of Mycenae should not have been shattered, in that time of troubles, by new Greek invaders.

Bronze cauldron, China; axe, Luristan; Hallstatt burial urn, Poland; bronze knife-handle, China.

Early iron axe and dagger

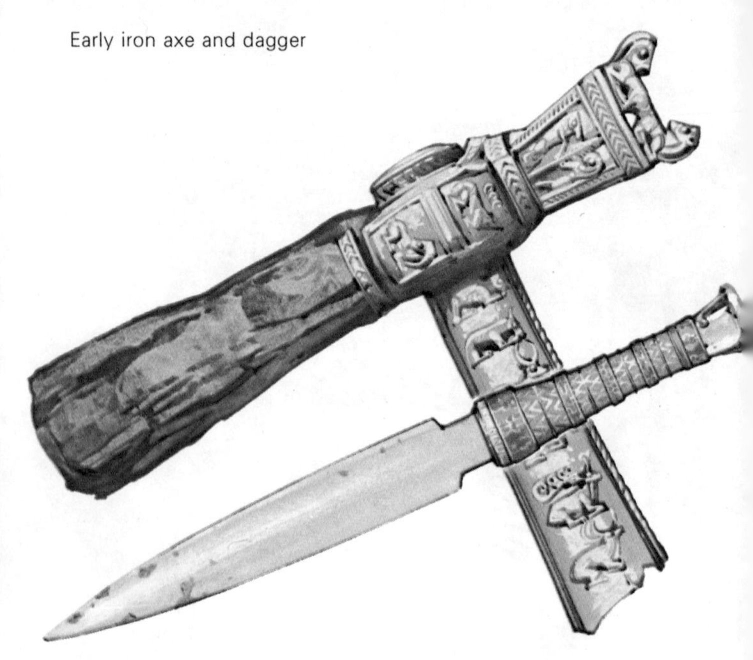

The coming of iron

In any generalized account the Iron Age is supposed to follow the Bronze Age as the latter is supposed to follow the Stone Age. But the beginnings of the Iron Age in various parts of the world are tricky to date partly because iron corrodes in soil much more than flint or bronze.

The coming of iron to each region of the world is astonishingly varied. In the Pacific a taste for iron was acquired by the scrounging of nails and other items from European expedition ships such as those of the eighteenth-century Captain James Cook. A European example from 500 B.C. or a little later might be a find from the Thames: a socketed iron axe which is a hammered, wrought version of late Bronze Age socketed axes of Europe.

No pattern of introduction is typical: in China, perhaps at the same time as the Thames axe was made, iron appears in a cast form and as a mould for bronze tools! As a further lesson in how human cultures vary we can recall that cast iron did not figure very much in European technology until the second half of the eighteenth century A.D.

Iron was used by Eskimos and by many other peoples in the form of worked meteoritic iron, which often contains an admixture of nickel that makes it most acceptable for tools. The smelting of iron ores was a later development. That copper ores were discovered before iron ores is not surprising since copper ores can be smelted by heat; iron ores need a good air blast and at first produce rough blooms that have to be hammered and reheated more than once. Hence the term 'wrought' iron.

In the past, prehistorians have with some reason assigned the period 1300–1200 B.C. as the main beginning of iron-working and the Iron Age proper in the Old World. But iron was worked a thousand years earlier: there is evidence that man was occasionally working iron in Anatolia and

Left, meteoritic iron. Right: iron tool edges, China

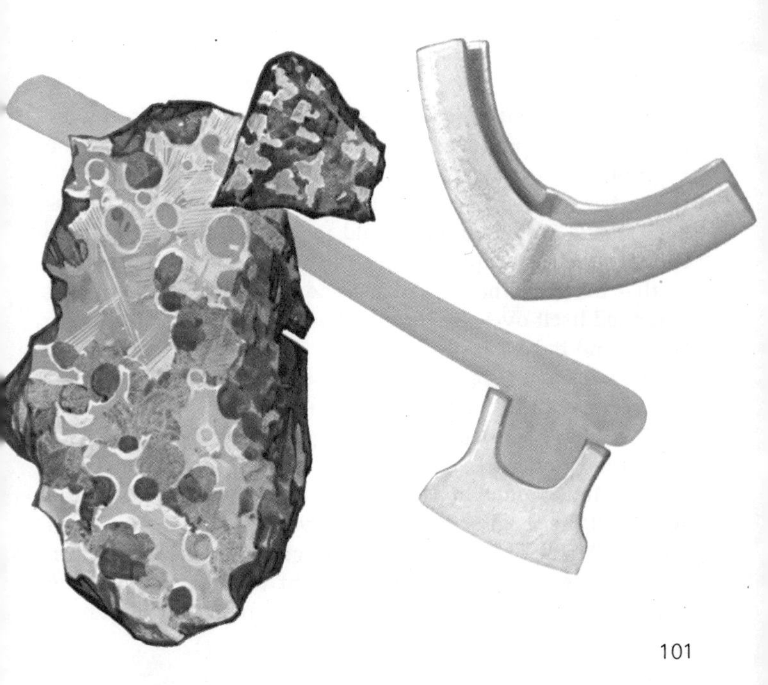

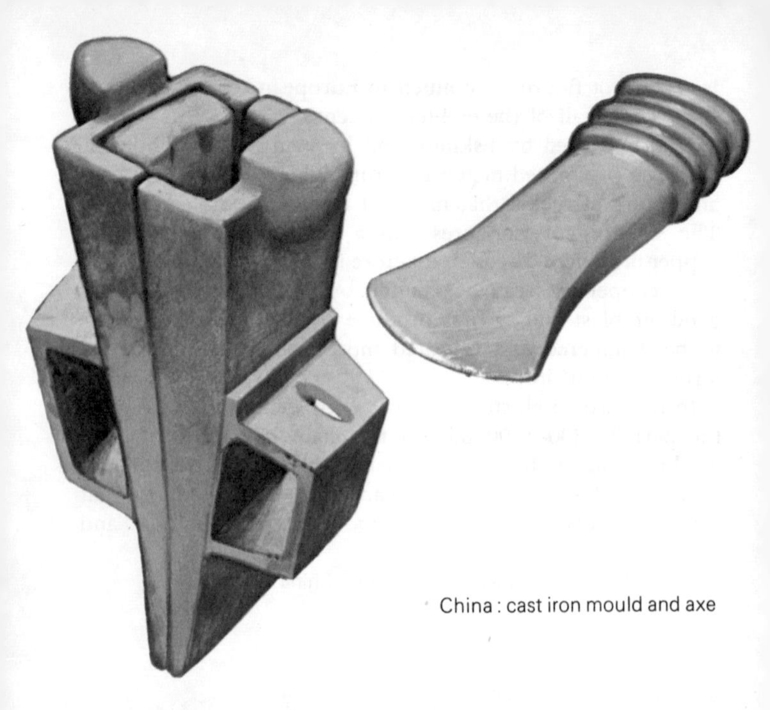

China : cast iron mould and axe

Mesopotamia and elsewhere. Properly wrought iron was being skilfully produced in the mountains of Armenia by the beginning of the second millennium B.C. Around 1500 B.C. in the lands ruled by the Hittites of Asia Minor an iron was being made which could be said to have steel-like qualities. Quickly the technique of selecting and working ores spread so that between the years 1200 and 1000 B.C. iron-working extended itself over the Near East as far as Persia as well as to Greece and Italy.

The ancient Egyptians used iron sporadically but they did not become an 'Iron Age culture' until about 700 B.C. They may well have learned iron-working long after the Phoenicians of Tyre, Sidon and Carthage. Iron spread into Africa very slowly. It is said that North Africa did not enter the Iron Age until the third or fourth century B.C. while the southern part of Africa did not achieve the general working of iron until the period A.D. 100–600. Recent work on radiocarbon dating in Africa has led to hypotheses that iron may have been used or worked in Africa as early as 900 B.C. African archaeology will supply many surprises for prehistorians.

In Europe the main impulse for iron-working followed the growth after 700–600 B.C. of the area around Hallstatt in Austria where suitable ores were available. Most of the Iron Age cultures of Europe owe something to Hallstatt.

Iron is thought to have come into general use in India at about the same time as Northern Europe, that is after 500 B.C., and in China a little later. However, there is always the probability of new discoveries which will show that there were sporadic introductions before that date. It has been noted that iron was in use in one place in India about 1000 B.C. This is still uncertain, but there is no doubt that India's skill in iron-working developed steadily. The Romans imported ingots of high-grade iron from India. Iron-working always maintained a regional air and technological advances were never widespread, even in the Middle Ages. The next moves forward in the technology of iron did not take place until the eighteenth and nineteenth centuries.

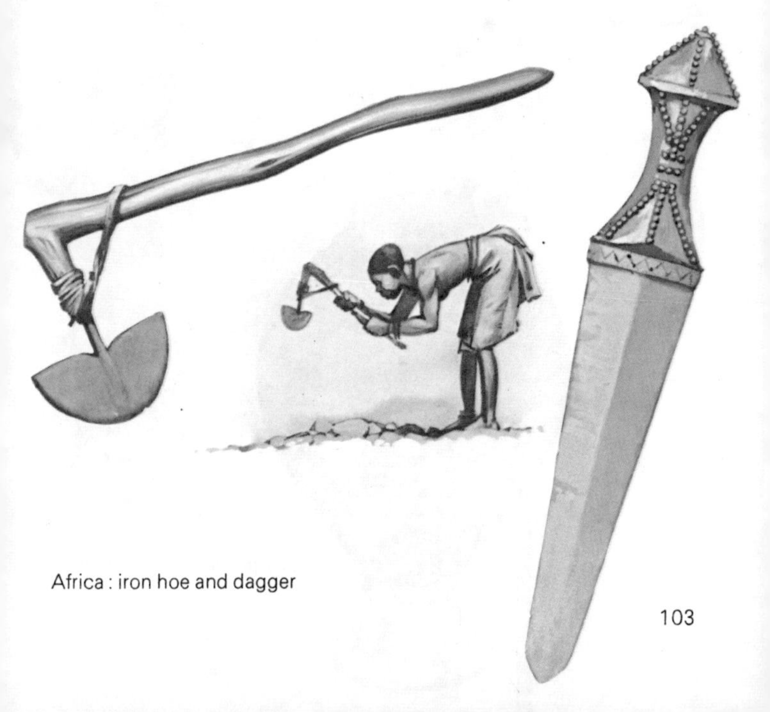

Africa : iron hoe and dagger

Early iron using cultures of Europe

The introduction of iron to Europe was not sudden. What really happened was that Bronze Age cultures of Europe gradually began to obtain iron implements or weapons. After the collapse of the Hittite empire in Asia Minor early in the 12th century B.C. the use of iron spread south into Palestine and westwards into Greece and the rest of south-east Europe.

By the end of the 9th century B.C. the so-called Urnfield cultures were reaching their maximum expansion in Central Europe. For convenience archaeologists use the omnibus term 'Hallstatt Culture' to describe the way of life and equipment of many European peoples. Hallstatt is a place near Salzburg where there were copper and salt mines – ideal if you wanted trade and influence. This centre was a natural place for developing the use of the new metal. There are many objects found in other parts of Europe, from Russia to Britain which

Iron Age tools and weapons, clay pot and bronze flagon

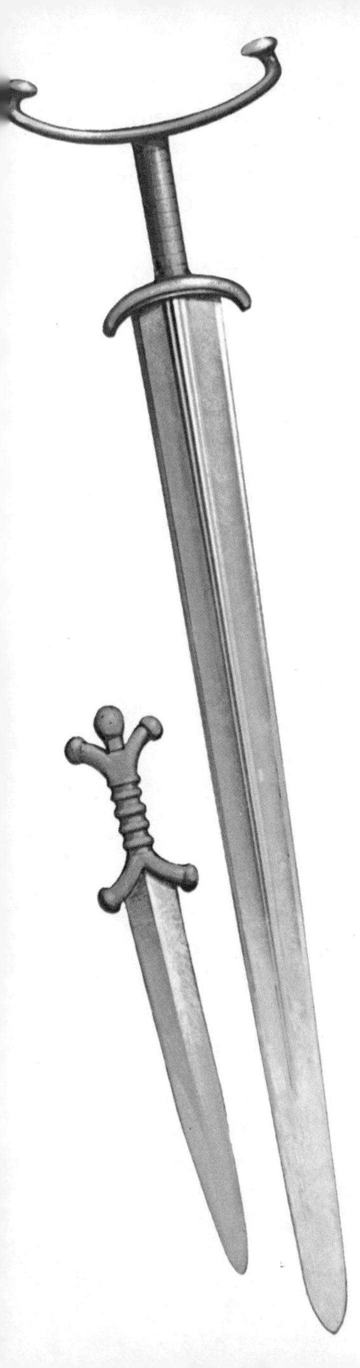

are labelled 'Hallstatt': bowls, razors, swords, wagons, pottery, hillforts, and the like. Much of the concentration of such objects is in east France and Germany. It was among Hallstatt folk of this area that in the period 600–400 B.C. the use of iron spread to the rest of Europe. The people concerned were in some cases Celtic speaking, but this does not mean that all Hallstatt culture users or iron users were Celts.

The reader must realize that titles like 'Hallstatt' are useful terms for grouping cultural features of one period – but an Iron Age warrior in many parts of Europe would have been very startled to be told he was a Hallstatt' warrior! A similar term used by archaeologists is 'La Tène culture' which comes from aspects of an art style of the late 5th century B.C. which are common to La Tène in Switzerland, where finds were made, and many parts of Europe from Scotland to Italy.

Perhaps the most important feature of the iron-using cultures of Europe is their contact with the Greek and Roman world.

Hallstatt swords

Aspects of the Iron Age in Europe

The words 'Iron Age' can be meaningless for many parts of Europe. They rarely imply a definite date; indeed many Iron Age peoples sometimes used very little iron, even though some iron may have been smelted in Central Europe even as early as 1800 B.C.

In many ways the most familiar European site in the annals of the Iron Age is Hallstatt in Austria. The Hallstatt cultures of France, Germany, Central and Eastern Europe show evidence of Greek influences.

By the sixth or fifth century B.C. the heyday of Hallstatt was over and the 'Celts' began to make nuisances of themselves all over Europe, and even penetrated into Asia Minor. The Celts had a distinctive art of their own which also owed something to the classical world. The type of site that gave its name to the art and techniques of the period is La Tène in Lake Neuchâtel in Switzerland, where quantities of distinctively decorated objects were found. This art can loosely be

A place of worship

Celtic art from Britain, France and Germany

called Celtic. Actually the original 'home' of the La Tène style was in areas near the Rhine.

The cultures of Iron Age peoples in Europe include such features the great earth-rampart forts with timber lacings found from Scotland to Germany; one may mention too the custom of burials with carts, excavated in Yorkshire, France and Central Europe. Also to be commented on is the use of coins (which were imitations of Greek ones) in the last two centuries B.C. and even the use of a modified alphabet (some Druids kept records).

The hillforts of Britain, the remarkable bronze shields and swords from the Thames, the astonishing gold or bronze collars of the British Iron Age as well as villages like Glastonbury or Little Woodbury, show what a varied culture there was in pre-Roman Britain.

CIVILIZATIONS AND THEIR DOWNFALLS

Some pre-Roman civilizations of the Mediterranean area

There is no place here to describe the long-lived culture of the Egyptians which, despite conquerors, survived at least 4000 years until Caesar's day. Even for the archaeologist who is not an Egyptologist, Egyptian finds in Europe have still been important in dating Greek and Bronze Age sites.

The Phoenicians a people of Semitic origin, are credited with introducing writing to the Greeks and subsequently, via the Romans to us. They were the first navigators to go through the straits of Gibraltar and to have circumnavigated Africa and reached the 'Tin Isles' of the north-west. Setting off from cities like Tyre and Sidon (northern Lebanon) they founded great colonies like Carthage. Tyre fell to Alexander in 332 B.C. and Carthage to the Romans in 146 B.C.

Though the Greek heritage to us has been an intellectual one, the archaeologist sees the hand of the Greek (or Hellene) in many things: in municipal architecture of many continents, in the smile and style of a Buddha in a part of India ruled by Greek kings; in the garbled patterns of Iron Age coins in Germany, France and England, which had been copied from copies of copies of Greek coins; in the leaf designs of a Greek-influenced Etruscan pot exported to France. Greece (or Hellas) was not so much the present Greece but a spread of

Figurines from Cyprus, Spain (Phoenician) and Syria

Civilization depends on trade

Etruscan wheeled object

Greek pot

settlers and colonies from the Black Sea and Asia Minor to France and Spain. Sicily and Southern Italy were sometimes known as Great Greece because of the number of Greek colonies. The great times of the Greek world, and especially of Athens, were the 8th century B.C. to 133 B.C.

Between 650 and 450 B.C. the Etruscans in the 'leg' of Italy were a most powerful people. In some respects, such as their art, they were influenced by the Greeks. For centuries their well appointed tombs have been the target of both archaeologists and looters.

The Romans as an Iron Age people

The Roman world of Scipio, Caesar and Marcus Aurelius has a unity that goes beyond the use of the Latin language. The influence of the Romans as in literature, law, and many aspects of life is a cliché of history. But Roman culture, if we include the world and times of Justinian lasted almost a thousand years and it underwent many changes. The archaeologist cannot assume that Roman institutions and artefacts remained the same during that time.

First it should be recalled that the Romans who came on the scene and settled in Alban Hills around the 10th century B.C. were just another early Iron Age (or even late Bronze Age) people. Right to the end of the Roman Empire the Romans borrowed from the peoples around them, ship designs, weapons, even deities. They were not always the most technologically advanced people; their iron tools and weapons were quite often inferior to those of the barbarians they fought or ruled. Perhaps the strength of the Romans was in their capability in organizing and using external elements. In Britain they burnt coal; in the Near East they borrowed cavalry techniques; in Rome they learned to wear (and pay for) the costly silks of China; they learned that their strength was in making external peoples want to become Romans. At the apex of the Roman Empire an emperor might be a Spaniard or a Berber or an Arab. Throughout most of its history Rome learned more from Greece than it ever taught.

It is said that it was in civil engineering and law that the Romans excelled other peoples. So it is for their use of concrete, or for their tolerance of the customs of other peoples;

customs and laws which they married with their own that we admire the Romans. While Rome copied much, we must not forget how she indirectly influenced peoples. In Britain some designs on pots show a mingling of Roman and 'Celtic' styles. Roman influence is seen in the shape of pottery of nations outside the Roman Empire as in Czechoslovakia.

Roman penetration to those parts was often in the nature of political infiltration or showing the flag. But 'Roman'

Left: a Roman hoist, 1st cent. A.D.

trade went everywhere; it did not always come from Rome but went from one part of the empire to another. For example 'Samian' or 'Terra Sigillata' ware made in France or West Germany and was exported in Britain, Poland, Sweden and elsewhere. To China went Roman trade missions from Syria and from Italy Amphorae and Arretine ware reached India. Roman objects in Thailand or Vietnam prove little.

The Roman world

The glorious age of the Roman Empire did not come into being until after the battle of Actium in 31 B.C. but Rome had begun to have an empire with dependent territories centuries before. Thus there were colonies and 'protectorates' long before the times of Caesar and Augustus and Rome's authority was spread from Spain to Asia Minor. But one should not forget another potent influence on Rome itself. When Rome

Aqueduct in Spain. Below: Hadrian's Wall

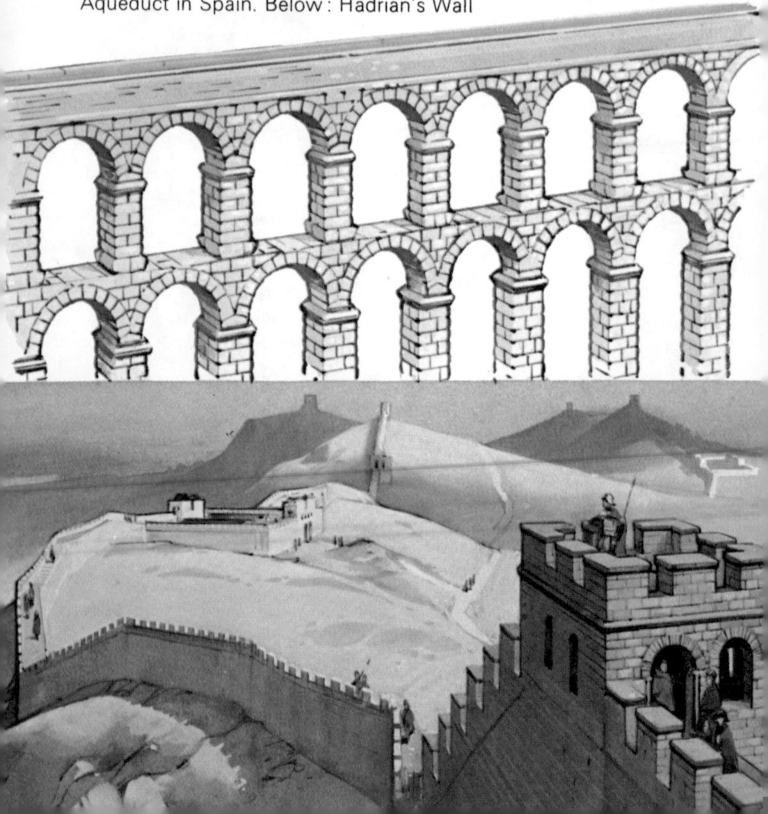

Pot from Northants. Coin of Honorius. Mosaic

took over most parts of the Greek-speaking world in the 2nd century B.C. she was in turn taken over in part by Greek cultures. Besides getting Greek philosophers and litterateurs to come over to teach young Romans, there were Greek technicians and artists being set to work by Romans. Often, therefore, an archaeologist may excavate a piece of Greek-influenced art whether in Africa or Romania (truly a Roman name) or Britain and will be faced with sorting out whether it is Roman (most likely) or Greek (not so likely).

The Roman influence on her empire so often merges with that of her subjects that it is hard to distinguish one from the other. A pot found at Meroe (modern Sudan) has a shape which is not Roman, but the slip pattern on it is one that can be seen in Britain or Germany. Though the Romans had sent a military expedition nearly a thousand miles to Meroe, most Roman objects will have been acquired by peaceable trade.

The Romans were great adaptors of religions, equipment and attire. They got silk from China and overcoats and baskets from Britain. In return they provided stability and resisted the periodic incursions of the barbarians.

Post-Roman migrations

In prehistoric times there were periods of unrest and movement, such as those of around 1200 B.C. and the largely Celtic movements across Europe between 500 and 100 B.C. But few had such a varied impact as the great 'migrations' that took place largely between the second half of the 4th century A.D. and (to close with an arbitrary point of relative quiet) 600 A.D. Generally food shortages, climatic changes and political vacuums have been suggested as reasons for these shifts of population.

In the 5th century A.D. 'Jutes', 'Angles' and 'Saxons' from areas between the mouths of the Rhine and the Oder, added themselves vigorously to previous Teutonic arrivals in a Britain no longer run by Rome. But they were not the first peoples to be on the move. Already, between about A.D. 375 and 454, the Huns had trampled their way across East and Central Europe. Around the same time, a Germanic people from the areas near the south shores of the Baltic, the Burgundians, began their warlike migrations.

The Vandals wandered from the Danube lands to Germany. By 409 they, and other peoples, had reached Spain. Twenty years later they crossed the straits to form a North African empire. From Carthage they sacked Rome in 455.

The Goths left the Baltic areas about the 2nd century A.D. and moved to near the Black Sea. They split and one group, the Visigoths, spread west in the 4th century and defeated the Romans more than once. Beaten by the Franks in 507 they finally contained themselves in Spain. The other more Eastern group, the Ostrogoths, willy-nilly mingled their fortunes with the Huns for a time, but finally left Hungary to set up an empire in Italy that lasted from 493 to the 550s when they were defeated by generals from Constantinople.

The groups mentioned above were a few among many others, such as the Germanic Lombards (6th century), or the Franks from the Rhineland who rose to power in the 5th and 6th centuries and made themselves into the first stable post-Roman state. Much later Europe was disturbed by one of the last of the vigorous migration peoples, the 'Norsemen' or 'Vikings' who from the end of the 8th century onwards stirred the world from Iceland to Russia.

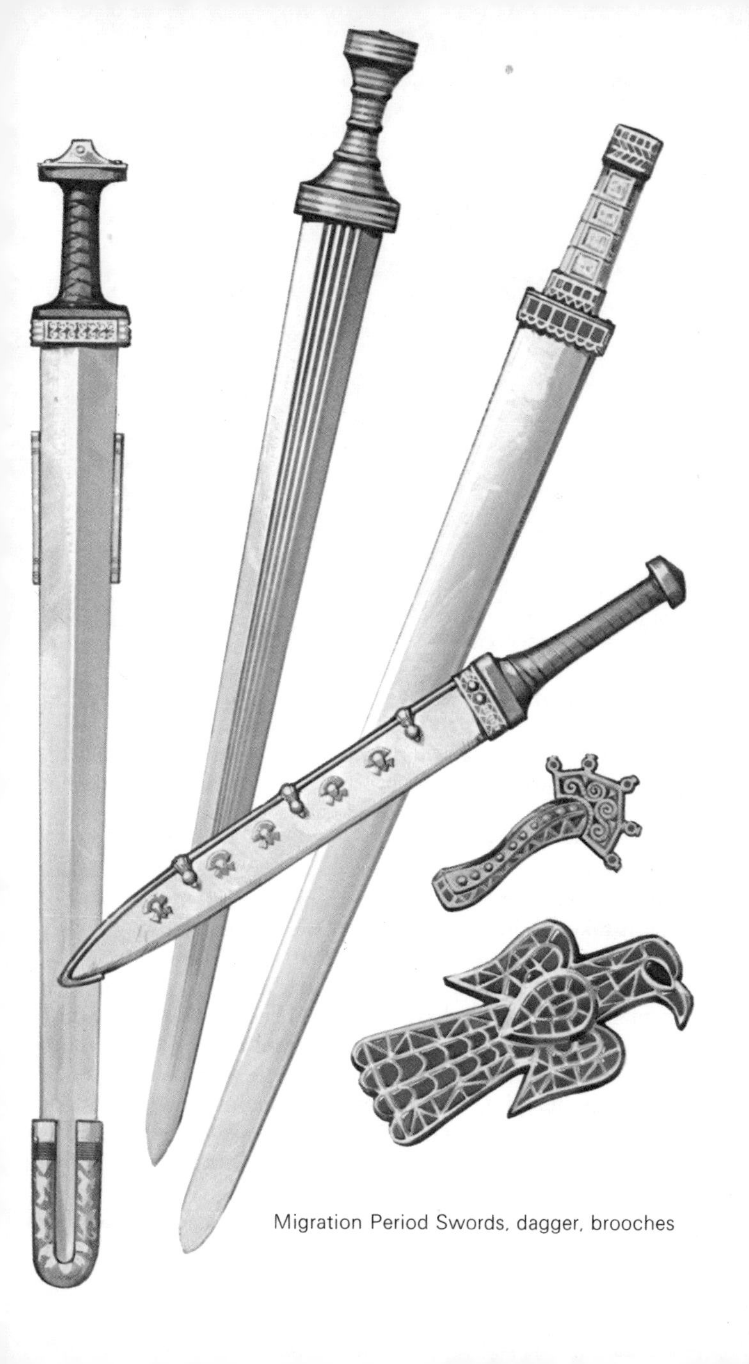

Migration Period Swords, dagger, brooches

Civilizations

The explorer who 'gets back to civilization' (i.e. hot baths, modern technological aids etc.) is sure that he is 'civilized'. Clearly the word 'civilization' is a tricky one and this is not helped by the layman's usage when he says, that 'archaeologists look for lost civilizations'.

Most groups of people have a way of life which distinguishes them entirely or partly from other groups. If 'way of life' is taken to include all one's material possessions, all one's mental and spiritual actions and attitudes, plus our social behaviour and structure, the sum of this behaviour we learn from our fellows is defined by archaeologists as a *culture*. When a culture of the past is elaborate and powerful, with centralized control, where, usually, there is writing, fine buildings, temples, monuments, systems of communications or economic organization such as roads or canals, it is conveniently said that we have a 'civilization'. But it is a scholar's convention.

Civilizations cannot begin until after the Neolithic way of

life has been established so that an agricultural or cattle owning system supplies a firm basis for the next important feature in several civilizations: trade.

Civilizations came and went. Sometimes they rose for 'obvious' geographical reasons; those of Egypt and Mesopotamia because of the fertility of the Nile, Tigris and Euphrates. Many civilizations fell by conquest, though some decayed internally and crumbled or were nibbled away from outside. Arnold Toynbee's *A Study of History* is a valiant attempt to solve, among other things, the unsolvable problem of the rise and fall of civilizations.

Civilizations can rise independently of each other as did those of the Old and New Worlds or they can influence each other as did those of Greece and Rome. More 'civilizations' in the broadest sense of the term will yet be found in the Neolithic of the Near East possibly and in the Far East; a few more 'civilizations' may be found in Africa and America.

Left: a popular idea of Egypt
Above: a Maya site
Right: Machu Picchu, Peru, discovered in 1911

Archaeology: present and future

What will the archaeologist of the future be like? His training will be more severe in detail and practice and he may not be allowed to specialize in one period too early. Today the archaeologist is an individual, in the future he will be part of a carefully selected team.

It is hoped that the archaeologist of the 21st century will have a wider organization to help him: trained workmen, draughtsmen, technicians, photographers and recording staff, a helicopter to survey sites, mobile and static laboratories and storage centres for analyzing finds.

With growing understanding of scientific aids digging will be brisker and perfectly problem oriented. The information at the digger's fingertips will be prodigious. All archaeological literature will have been put into abstract form and stored in a computer memory. A telex message to a record centre will answer for him questions like 'At what salt-pan sites, anywhere in the world have semi-circular support bars of earthenware been found?' Within seconds (and this is no exaggeration) the output printer of a computer at base will print out a list of classified sites and finds. A photo-printer attached to the apparatus will a few minutes later slide out

Archaeology should not operate on a shoestring

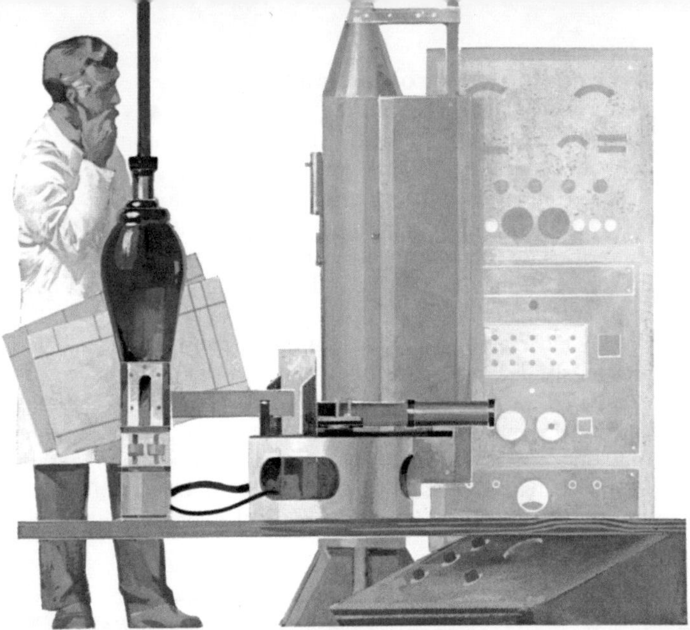

Equipment is not enough : collaboration is essential

automatic xerox-copies of articles offering parallels to the finds the archaeologist has just dug. A sketch of a pot scanned with a phototracer can be made to compare itself automatically with drawings of similar pots in museums elsewhere in the world. Utopian ? No, all the techniques exist to carry out the above. But the archaeologist cannot do this without paying a personal price. He cannot keep his own index of specialities, he has to share his knowledge quickly. Rewards of collaboration are greater than those of personal hoarding.

At the moment archaeology is undergoing a crisis of identity. It uses so many other disciplines that some outsiders have said that it is not a subject in its own right. This is a criticism that has been levelled at geography and other broad disciplines. Yet most people want to know more about mankind's past and if archaeology can cease to borrow uncritically ideas from anthropology, linguistics, sociology and other subjects, it can become a powerful tool for understanding the growth of man into the future. The great peril is that the growth of archaeology may be stunted today.

Archaeological problems and ethics

The archaeologists must not dig just to 'see what's under that mound'. He must be able to prove that he is doing a dig to solve a properly posed problem.

Sometimes the archaeologist is called in to do an 'emergency' or 'rescue' dig because a site is threatened. While he is entitled to dig with promptness a site that is going to disappear, it may be that he is doing a dig which could have been anticipated by a well-planned policy.

All excavation is destruction. Many archaeologists religiously leave a part of a site, especially a cave, unexcavated so that future workers with superior techniques can have some sort of comeback. Another school believes that one can leave too large an area unexcavated, thereby losing valuable clues. There is much to be said for total excavation, but there is a problem for the conscience: has the

Below: a professional problem-centred dig

excavator the time, storage space, equipment, staff and broad approach that will enable him to write a report on his total excavation?

Quantities of material, such as pottery, once excavated present great problems. Is the digger to 'select' important pieces without elaborate statistical techniques? What museum can afford the foresight to plan sorting depots and stores for material waiting to be 'selected'?

At every point the professional archaeologist has to make decisions and exercise judgments that will affect the researchers of the future. His recording, his storage his relations with other scholars must be perfect. The amateur archaeologist must not dig for curiosity; he must not maintain private collections when they should be in museums; he must be prepared to help recover the archaeology of his region even if it is of a period he does not find glamorous.

Below: CHAOS from poor direction and untrained people

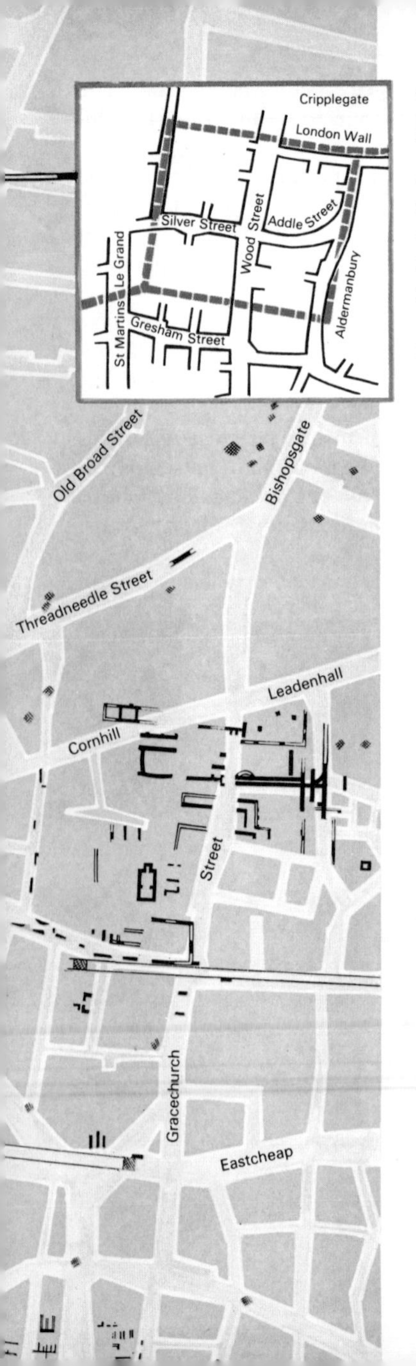

Archaeological prospecting (1)

While it is a matter of ancient faith that the best archaeological exploration is done on foot, it is foolish to ignore the help that comes from maps old and new, air photographs and the various methods of geo-physical prospecting.

The most modern of large-scale maps may show by the way that fields are arranged, or by the patterns of areas uncultivated because of large stones, ancient roads or settlements which can be discovered in the study – as long as things are verified on the ground.

An old estate map, one or more centuries old, may have features on it which are today completely buried and certainly completely unrecognizable from a modern map. However, it is not the antiquity of a map that matters, nor its details, but the interpretation put on it. Though the ins-and-outs of the line of the Roman wall of London were well known, it was not until after the Second World War that an archaeologist was able to

Modern London Streets follow the lines of the Roman fort and town

point out that the north-west corner marked the outline of a Roman military fort which had been built before the walls of London had been erected.

Air photographs, depending on the time of year and day they are taken, can show the archaeologist anything from a buried city to a small group of burials. Though air photographs can bring out details of low features because of the shadows at the extremes of a day, most ancient features show up at certain times because of changes in vegetation. A wall buried a little below the surface will make the soil above it shallow, with a corresponding thinning or lighting-up of the grass or vegetation. Similarly a ditch, filled in during the centuries will offer a deeper soil with a corresponding lusher vegetation for the aerial observer to see.

The study of air photographs requires a growing body of techniques nowadays: the sophisticated use of stereoscopes and photogrammetric (maps from air photos) equipment.

Ring ditches of causewayed camp showing in a cabbage field

A proton magnetometer

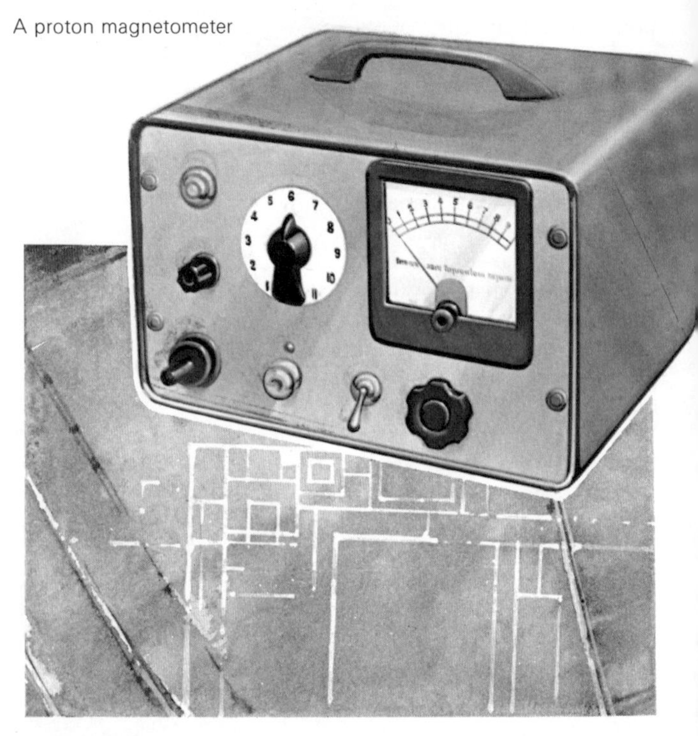

Archaeological prospecting (2)

Since 1945 scientific methods of prospecting in the field have made considerable advances. The main problem is to choose the appropriate apparatus for a particular job. Apparatus can sometimes be costly but it has been found that small museums or amateur societies have always been able to devise cheaper forms of equipment. There are two main groups of prospecting equipment though, doubtless, other types, radically different are being developed as these words are being written. The broad groups are (a) the resistivity meters, and (b) magnetometers such as the proton magnetometer and the proton gradiometer.

The resistivity meter is based on the fact that the ground can conduct electricity. Different soils or rocks conduct differently. It is clear then that probes linked with a meter placed in the ground will register a certain amount of flow in ordinary earth, but will register differently if a buried wall or filled ditch alters the resistivity of the soil. This kind of apparatus is suited for problems like 'does the wall seen in this excavated area continue below surface to that end of the field?' Much excavation can be saved if the wall (or a road, or a building) can be picked up further on.

The magnetometer is a sophisticated apparatus which has been found useful in detecting buried iron, kiln sites and rubbish pits with certain kinds of soil. The magnetometer detects *anomalies* or contrasts between the general magnetic field of an area and that above or near a buried object or a kiln several feet below. The instrument is very sensitive and can detect a difference in the field of the ratio one to 70,000. Its very sensitivity can be an inconvenience: a large penknife or a bunch of keys in the pockets of a person holding the detector can give a false reading. A car or a train or electricity pylons too near the equipment can also induce errors.

Surveying with a proton magnetomater

The body of Anne Mowbray, Duchess of York, was found by chance on a Stepney bomb-site in London. River surveys have proved very useful to the archaeologist.

Enterprise and rescue on land and water
On Land

Many discoveries are made by accident during building operations. Though there are laws in most countries relating to the saving of antiquities, contractors regard the archaeologist as an expensive nuisance who stops work.

An efficient archaeologist should be able to anticipate future discoveries from past frequencies of finds in the vicinity. By establishing good public relations with landowners, civil engineers, contractors, agents, clerks of work, builders, foremen and workmen, he can find it easy to persuade them to notice objects and to report them with the understanding that the archaeologist will not create embarrassment for his informants. An archaeologist must not break trust after an agreement is made; once he breaks faith informants may become clam-like. As in the world of spy fiction the rescue-archaeologist, even though he may be an official, has sometimes to make unofficial deals for the sake of winning future knowledge, that must appear officially and academically reprehensible. Sometimes he has to forego access to one site to win access to many other sites.

By Water

Underwater archaeology is to the serious scholar both a delight and a source of distress. From the findings of gold ritual objects in the great sacred well at Chichen Itza in Yucatan, Mexico, to the raising of the 17th-century ship *Vasa* off Sweden, under-water archaeology has excited the world. Shiploads of ancient goods have been found: a scattered cargo of Roman 'Samian' ware off the coast of Kent, or a Bronze Age vessel loaded with ingots, scrap and implements of about 1200 B.C. found off Cape Gelidonya, Turkey. Groups of contemporary objects such as are found in a ship's hold are invaluable as dating evidence.

But time and time again objects have been taken irrevocably out of context by divers archaeologically inexperienced or archaeologists with inadequate sub-aqua experience.

The archaeologist needs the good will of all

The hunt for clues

No archaeologist will have time to walk over every corner of his 'territory'. Even if he has maps, air photographs and good local contacts he cannot spot everything himself. What clues must he teach himself and his informants to use? No example of any clue will apply to every part of the world. In temperate countries, the nettle (*Urtica dioica*) seen in a lonely spot may indicate past human occupation. A field might show by a ring of nettles the presence of the filled ditch of a burial barrow. In America sage (*Salvia subincisa*) has turned up significantly at pre-Colombian ruin sites.

But botanical clues are just a few among a thousand possible clues. A British archaeologist sees Norse place-names in Lancashire and tries to follow up the Viking history of the area. In Spain archaeologists note that one region has a concentration of place-names, Celtic ones. Conclusions about early Celtic settlements can then be made, especially if there are excavated finds of the 8th century B.C. that confirm the presence of such settlers.

Sometimes a distribution map may show up connections

Celtic place-names often give clues of prehistoric settlements

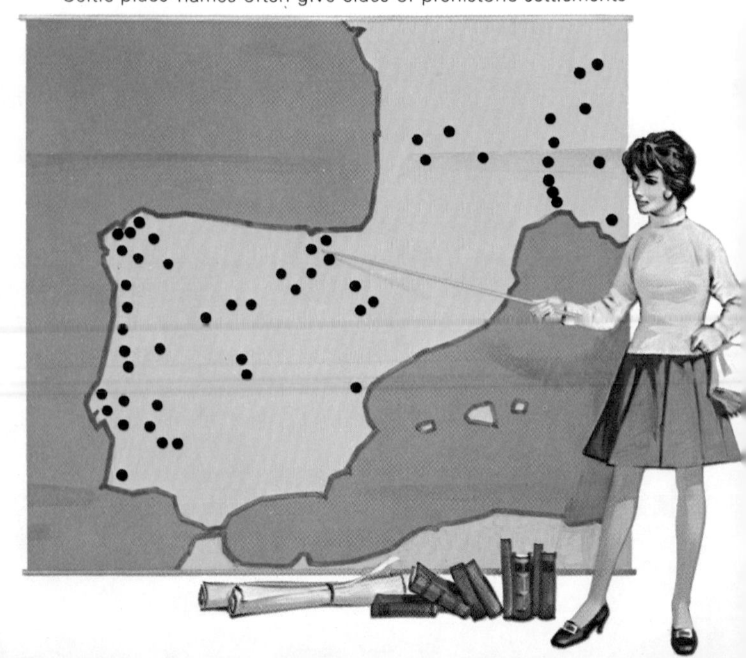

Certain plants offer clues about past settlements

that are not clear on the ground, but there are perils. An archaeologist finds that there are upright stone monuments at many places where Neolithic polished stone axes are found. In fact the coincidence is too good to be true. The standing stones may be of the Late Migration period or as late as the 10th century A.D. They are placed near settlements where soil was good, and this is where Neolithic man had been – three thousand years before.

One of the best examples of the good use of clues comes from the story of archaeological researches in India and Pakistan, before the coming of radiocarbon dating. Dating was accordingly difficult. A systematic survey was undertaken in many museums for *Roman* pots. Eventually a few were found, and the places where they were most plentiful were excavated until a layer was found with Roman pottery sherds in it, the layers above and below it were accordingly fixed relative to Roman times and a workable chronology began to be forged.

Survey and recording

The archaeologist, whether professional or amateur, has to learn the art of plotting finds and making plans of sites and digs. While he does not have to be a professional surveyor or mathematician, he must be familiar with the basic techniques of using survey tapes or chains, the surveying prismatic compass, the level, and the theodolite. In some terrains he will need to be able to use a plane-table.

Before he begins an excavation, or immediately after he has discovered a new site, the archaeologist must be able to carry out speedy surveys which can readily be transferred to paper or on to map plans. He has to have the judgement that chooses the correct standard of accuracy – it is no use measuring a wall-thickness to the nearest millimetre, if the drawn wall will be a thinly marked hair-line on a map.

The *level* is used for checking trench levels and relating a site and its layers to a standard datum level; it is essential for contours or for checking whether one end of a structure or level has subsided. Environmental archaeologists find the level invaluable for relating sites to ancient river terraces or shorelines.

The large surveying prismatic compass or the more accurate theodolite are the obvious instruments for preparing the ground plan of an excavation area or a group of structures. The theory of these instruments is easy to learn, but constant practice will be needed to ensure ease of handling. Such instruments will help on a survey to detect deviations from a right-angle of buildings or to fix a newly-discovered site in relation to known landmarks. If properly calibrated, the telescope of a theodolite will find the distance of a survey staff from the instrument.

The plane-table is at its best in large tracts of treeless country. The main landmarks in a thousand square miles can be plotted in an afternoon. There are several ways of using a plane table and old methods may still suit modern sites.

In the next decade new types of apparatus will make surveying even more automatic for the archaeologist.

Right, above: a surveyor's prismatic compass
Right, below: levelling with a staff

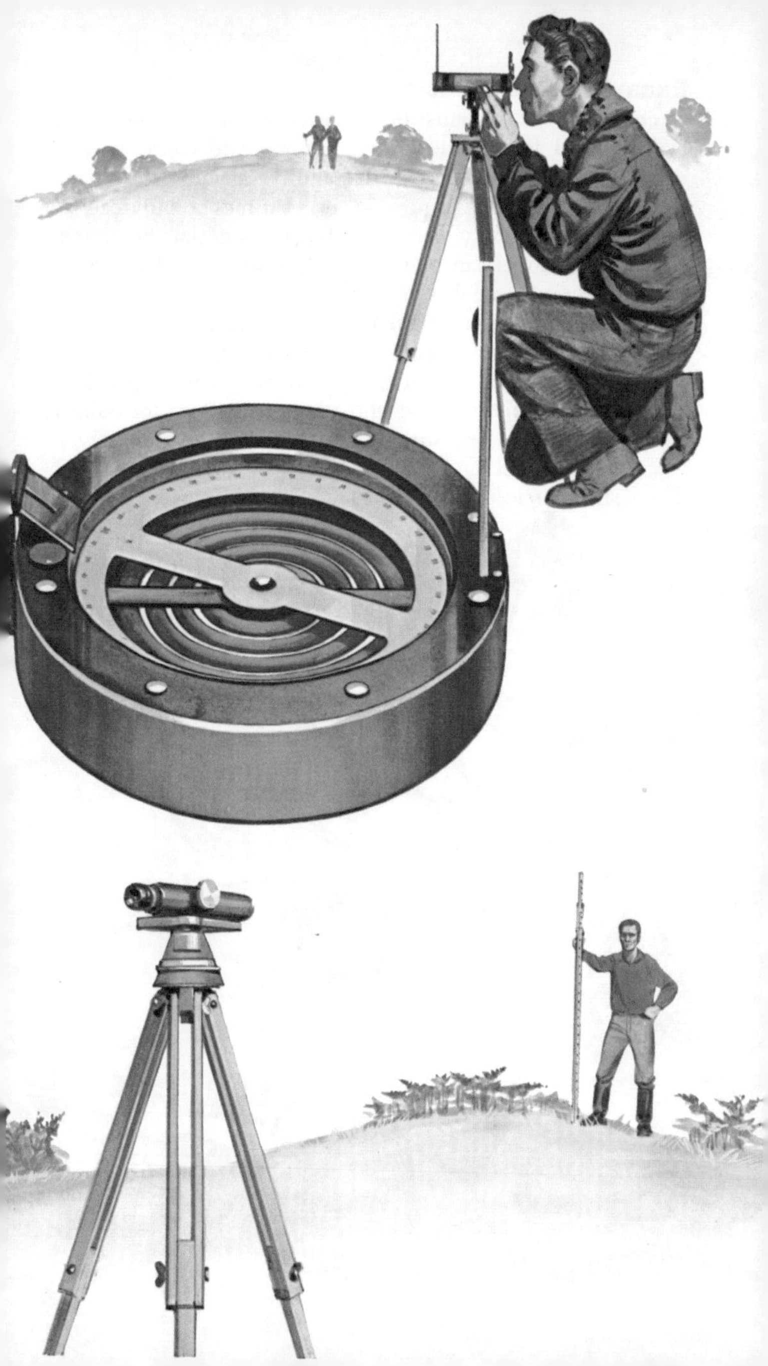

Excavation: the basic kit

Archaeological tools must be as varied as the many tasks that are required in an excavation. For delicate work, such as digging a skeleton, a small brush and the slenderest of dental probes seem almost crude. At other times a bulldozer to remove 19th-century urban rubble is essential. Sometimes a pick or a shovel can be used safely, but in most layers the smallest scraping tool is best. In many countries the brick-layer's pointed trowel is the most favoured tool.

The excavated and sifted soil must be removed promptly whether by manual labour or by a conveyer to a spoil heap which is conveniently near and yet not too near for danger. Elaborate safety precautions must be taken to prevent

The greater the variety of equipment the better

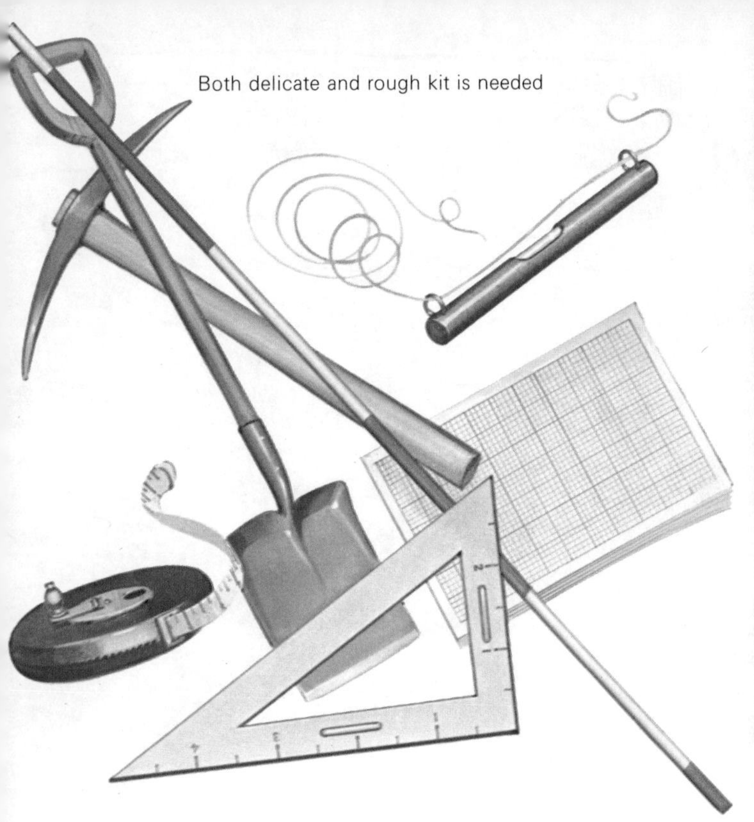
Both delicate and rough kit is needed

collapse. An efficient excavation has a variety of ingenious apparatus available: photographic towers, pumps, concrete breakers for urban sites, ladders and so on. Some excavators in rainy climes use giant polythene canopies. Obviously it is not possible to learn from books what is essential equipment.

In the British Isles and some other countries there are many excavations which are run by local societies which have competent excavators but may be handicapped by inadequate equipment. Each kind of excavation needs special equipment and this may require maintenance and repair during the months before the dig starts. Anticipation of difficulties is vital: have you got fencing adequate to deal with both children and animals? Have you the means to cope with mud? Has the tool-shed an adequate padlock?

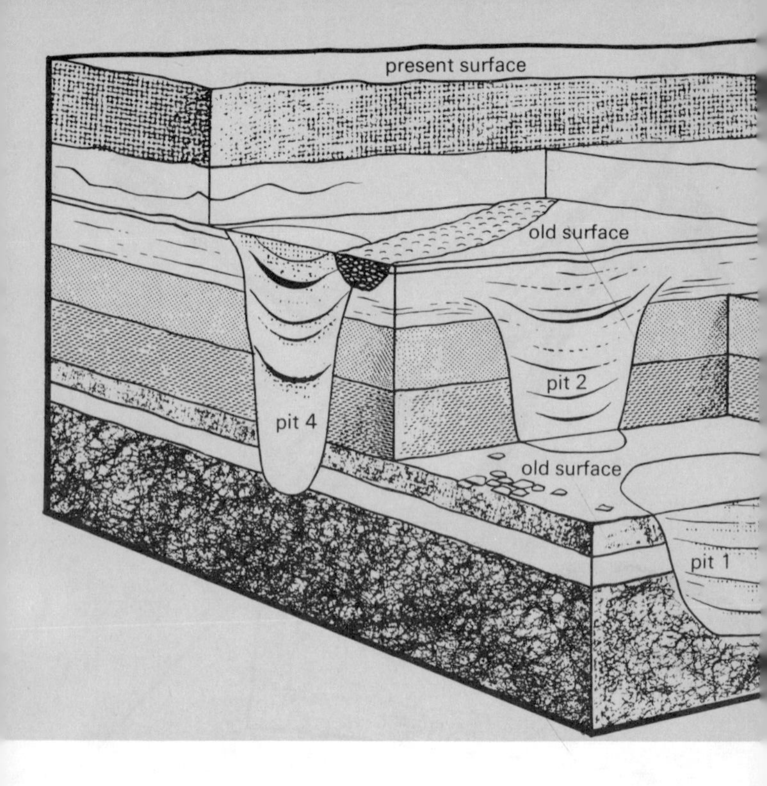

Excavation and sections

It is not the depth above sea-level at which an object was found that matters. The important thing is to know in what layer something was found, and, in addition, how and when the layer was deposited. This means that the finding of objects can, paradoxically, be less important than interpreting a layer. What good is it to find an artistic object and to run so inefficient a sitebook that you cannot assign it with certainty to a Roman or an Iron Age layer?

There are a thousand practicalities that go to the excavation of a site. No book can teach the skilful movement of a scraping tool which, in the hands of the digger, senses that a change in soil texture heralds the revealing of a new layer. No manual can adequately describe the techniques by which every detail of the layers is recorded interpretatively. It is

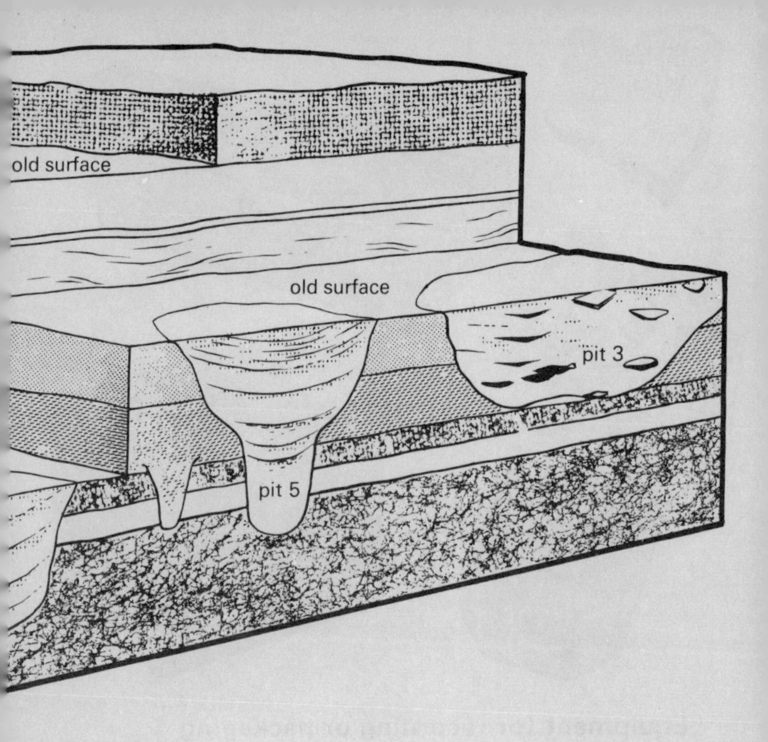

The layers in an excavation can often be more complicated than this

better to record how a layer lies and supply some knowledge of how it was formed than to describe its coloration in artistic detail. Nevertheless, a sharp eye must be kept on a layer at several stages of an excavation. At first it may be moist and sticky. A few days later it is a little dusty. Judicious scraping when the section is being drawn may reveal traces of charcoal or a general slope. Dense rootlet patterns may indicate where there once had been timber.

The excavator must draw all the layers, having numbered them physically with labels. The drawing should have all the layers numbered and, where possible, enough symbols or captions should go with the section drawing in order to assist the reader and enable him to grasp the full significance of all the layers.

Equipment for recording or packaging

Recording

Good excavation needs good recording. Meticulousness in recording is essential since a new find is so obvious to the eye that it seems unbelievable that in a few months time people who were present will disagree violently as to which way up it was.

Essentials for an excavation include:

(a) Large note book – a log of activities, with sketches in it.
(b) Layer labels (for marking excavated layers)
(c) Two labels similar to (b) to go with finds.
(d) Photographs. These must be documented serially or they are useless.
(e) Drawing board and good quality paper.
(f) Bags, boxes and crates: all to be well labelled.
(g) Marking of finds (best done in Indian ink or paints). If labels are used they must be firmly fixed.
(h) Numbering of finds e.g. AB1969/3834 which means this

is item 3834 of a series dug in 1969 at a site coded as 'AB'. There are many variants of this method.

(i) Finds record book. Each item must have source site area, layer, position etc., listed. Leave blank columns for comments or sketches. Note that some excavators prefer to use cards instead.

Make sure that jars, specimen tubes etc. have indelible labels inside as well as outside.

Packaging

An excavator should do what he can to have containers and packaging suitable for all eventualities.

Some finds to be kept moist on their way to a conservation laboratory, other items like sherds should be dry before putting into storage. Soils and many organic substances grow fungus quickly if incorrectly packed. Flints, prehistoric sherds and, indeed, all finds should be packed so that they do not rub or grate when travelling.

Left: use system to mark pots, labels, boxes etc.
Below: recording kit must be the best

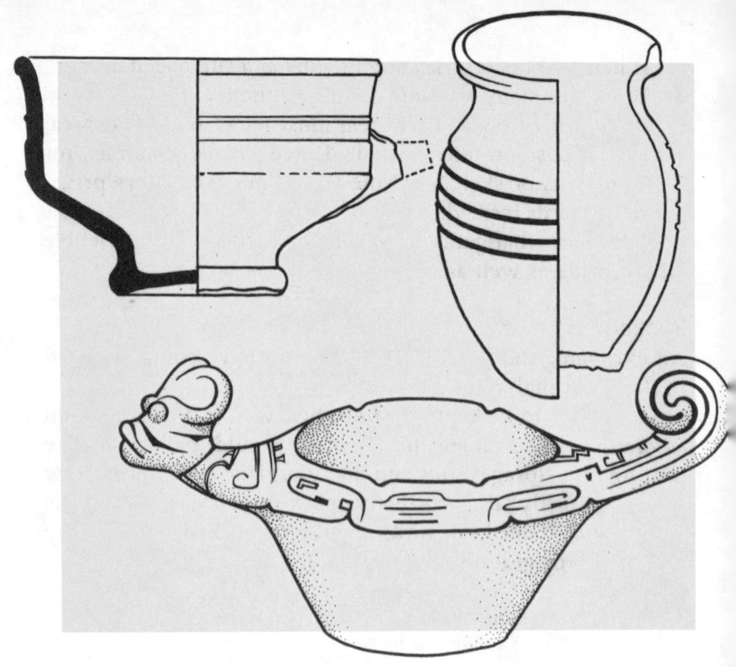

Some European and American conventions for drawing pots

Some archaeological drawing conventions

When objects are dug up it is often important to get good photographs made of them. Properly-taken photographs with scales, good lighting and the use of appropriate lenses and film are invaluable as records. But photographs are expensive and often a block made from a drawing in Indian ink will be more useful for comparisons than a photograph.

Special conventions have been devised for showing objects and their key dimensions. It is not likely that the conventions will become international, but each archaeologist tries to be consistent with his own practice and those of his colleagues in his own field.

Pots are usually shown 'half x-rayed'. Texture is only shown in special cases. Flint tools are shown with flake hollows indicated by inked lines. Other stone implements are often shown by stippling. Badly-corroded metal can also be shown by stippling since there is rarely any chance of confusion. Smooth metal is often rendered by a minimum of parallel hatchings.

There are many conventions for showing ground features like ditches or rising ground. These can be selected from the published practice of go-ahead archaeologists in various countries, but choose always the convention that uses the least amount of ink.

All drawings whether of Iron Age forts or Bronze Age pins should show cross-sections. A cross-section can be of diagnostic importance so do not assume your reader can guess at it. Do not hesitate to add neat captions and labels to your drawings so that they become self explanatory. Do not force the reader to flip back and forward among pages to get explanations of drawings.

Last but not least show a scale, preferably a linear scale rather than the statement 'all objects 1:2' or worse, 'scales 1:2 to 1:5'. All drawings in a report should, if possible, be numbered in an order that matches the sequence of the text.

Leather and metalwork illustrated

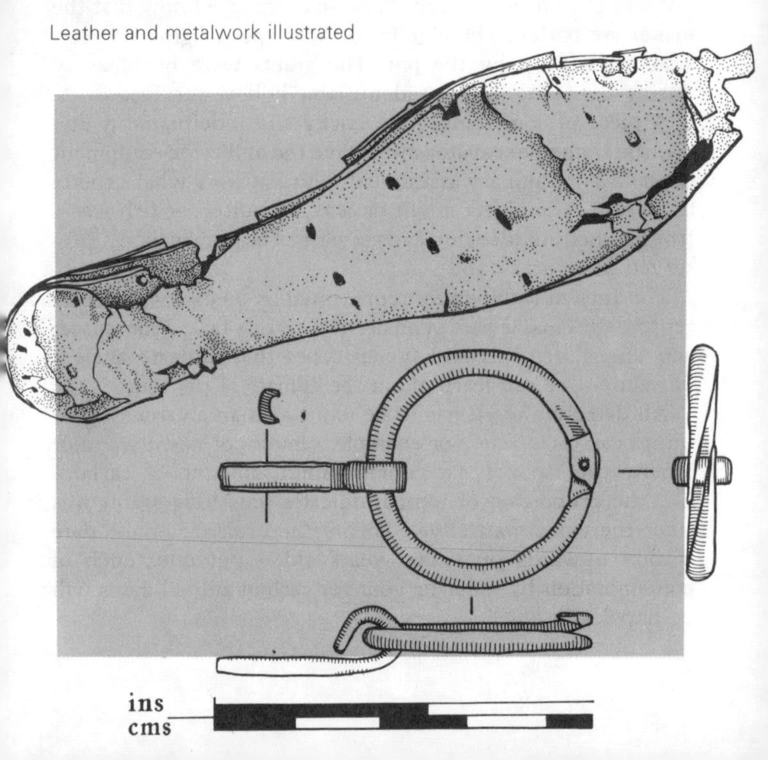

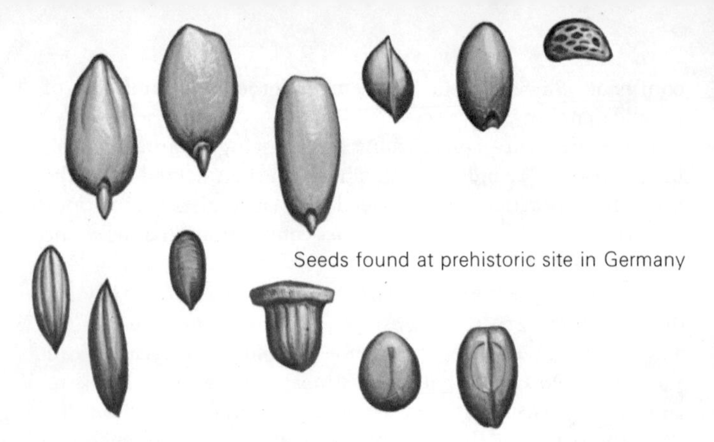

Seeds found at prehistoric site in Germany

Detective work

The systematic excavator cannot depend only on obvious finds such as pottery, tools, art objects and the like. He has to study *context* with the diligence that a detective brings to bear on a crime. Once, in the Neolithic period, a newly-made pot was put on the ground. Because of this we know that the maker ate barley. The clue from the shapes of grain impressions picked up by the pot. The grains were burnt away during the firing, but the identifiable hollow survived.

A piece of something grey, sticky and indefinable is dug up: the trained excavator must have the ability or equipment to make a preliminary assessment, plus knowing what experts to consult. The object might be wax, or butter, or fish-waste from a shell midden, or even a part of a human body preserved in an acidic soil!

The ancient *environment* represented by an excavated layer represents a major part of an archaeologist's task. From insect and animal remains and pollen types that indicate ancient vegetation, he can learn about the climate of the time.

All detective work has to be done with an awareness that things can go wrong. For example, samples of burnt wood or other carbon sources can contain minute amounts of 'carbon-14', the proportion of which indicates how long ago it was since the wood was 'alive'. This method can sometimes date carbon upwards of 30,000 years old – but one touch of contamination by older or younger carbon and all dates will be hopelessly out.

The scientist is daily using techniques that may be of use to the archaeologist, if the latter takes the trouble of learning some science. For example, bones buried in the ground take up over time small quantities of the element fluorine. Two bones buried at the same time in the same place should contain the same amount of fluorine. If a bone is introduced next to another that has been there a long time already, the intrusive bone will have less fluorine. This method of relative chronology is useful in detecting the faking of evidence (as for the Piltdown finds) or for checking whether a bone found in gravel is older than another with it.

Radiocarbon dating lab. The fluorine content increases with time

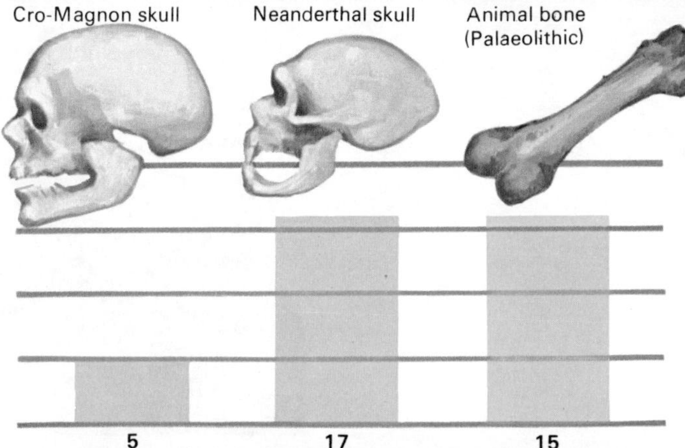

Dating by annual layers

Each year new methods of dating objects and deposits are hopefully announced. These approaches are so varied and require such elaborate apparatus and know-how that here it is better to discuss two techniques which have been used with reasonable success during the last fifty years: *tree-ring dating* and *varve chronology*.

Tree rings

Trees should produce a new ring each year. For various reasons (which are modified by climate, soil and the tree species) the rings vary in thickness. In a particular species of tree grown in one area there will be found a sequence of combinations of thick and thin which can be similar for trees of the same date, e.g. thick, thin, thick, thick, thin, thin. Let us describe this simply as + − + + − − and consider a recently cut stump which has, outwards from the centre, this sequence for the *first* eighteen years of its life: + − − − − − + + + + − − − − + − − − . . . and so on to the bark of this tree which is 200 years old. If nearby a roughly hewn beam is excavated or a barn timber is noted which has at one corner the sequence + − − − − + + + + − − − − + − − − and bark fragments, we can see that the similarity is exact and that the log was cut over 200 years ago. Subsequent finds of older beams will produce overlapping sequences which will help provide a dating sequence. Tree-ring dating has been

Tree-rings date a Russian town

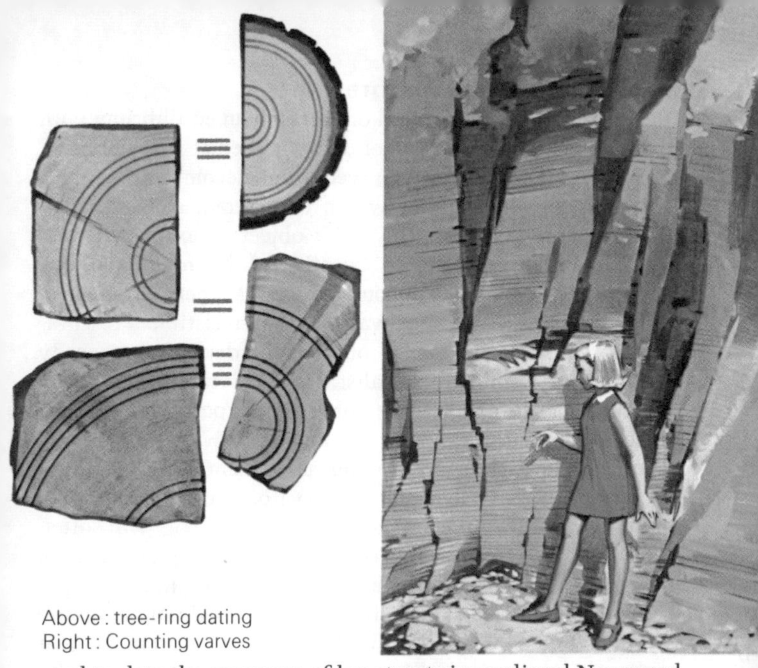

Above: tree-ring dating
Right: Counting varves

used to date the sequence of log streets in medieval Novgorod in the U.S.S.R. and to date American Indian sites that go back 2000 years.

Varves

Varve dating depends on the turbulent spring waters that come down from glaciated areas and deposit, at first, rough deposits in lakes but later, in the autumn, drop only the finest silt until all deposition stops in the winter. Each year a layer, or *varve,* is added. Varves vary in thickness and offer sequences that vary sufficiently to be analyzed like tree-rings. In certain lake-deposits of Scandinavia and North America it has been possible to count back (often using strings of adjacent lakes for overlaps) to either some year dated by a special inundation or right back to the period immediately after the last retreat of the glaciers.

Among the problems connected with dendro-chronology and varves is that in some years no new ring or layer is produced. Occasionally a tree can produce two rings in a season or a lake two or more varves in a year.

Conservation and restoration

Objects buried in the ground often reach an equilibrium with their environment. The rate of decay is then at a minimum. If the object is organic, it is saved from decomposition by a constant moisture content which may retain soil chemicals that help preservation. Once the object is excavated it is liable to lose water and to be affected by night and day temperature changes: decomposition is then often fast. Fungi and bacteria find excavated items irresistible. Preservation or conservation of an object will depend on speedy handling by a trained specialist. Careful wrapping to retain moisture may be of some use but with inexpert wrapping the object becomes a focal point for mould growth.

During the speedy and complex assessment of the condition of a find the archaeologist-conservator must consider the nature of the soil. An acid site, such as a peat bog, will soften the bones of a burial but preserve the flesh; an alkaline deposit, such as chalk, will keep only the bones intact.

Many organic substances like leather, wood, and cloth are restored by impregnation with chemical substances that replace the moisture-filling of cavities. Metals, especially iron and lead, are extremely difficult to preserve from further

break-down. Again, what seems to be a copper or bronze coin may be basically a silver one; the copper has 'migrated' to the outside and poses a pretty problem. Sometimes the corrosion products are removed by tools and sometimes by electrolysis. Preliminary x-ray of metal is recommended since even the most skilful cleaning may lose features such as inlays. An x-ray photograph will detect the patterns in the original metal even if every part of it is rust or verdigris.

Conservation to prevent deterioration is just one problem. Other problems arise since an object has to be made feasible for museum display or for study. This can be most difficult. Pots can be restored with plastic fibres or plaster and painted, but there is a sort of ethic which prevents the part mended from looking too much like the original. Otherwise one might draw false conclusions about the pot's character.

Writing-up and records

The archaeologist who has excavated a site has *destroyed* evidence. What he has dug cannot be put back for re-consideration. *Having dug he must publish,* however un-spectacular the results are. If no publisher or periodical can

A conservation laboratory

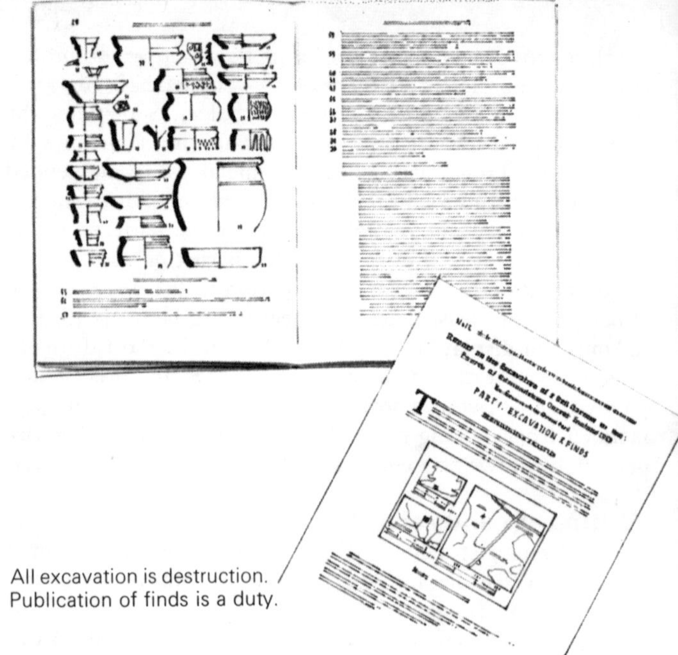

All excavation is destruction. Publication of finds is a duty.

find space for the results of a dig, the archaeologist should deposit a copy of his report and drawings in the regional museum. Printing costs are high nowadays, but many archaeologists are willing to forego the dignity of print and make their finds known in duplicated or offset-litho form.

A published report should have a short synopsis at the beginning or end. The report should be brief but not too cryptic or allusive. Most archaeological reports will be read in countries outside that of its origin, so the author has to be considerate when considering the obvious: there is a Santiago in Spain, one in Chile, one in Argentina, as well as one in Cuba. The county or province or district you work in will gain in fame from your writings – as long as you mention where it is. A good report will have key maps showing precisely where a site is.

A report should have illustrations of key objects drawn with enough systematic care to make them comparable with similar objects found in museums or other illustrations. However do not forget to include an accurate scale so that the reader will be able to see exactly what size an object is.

Throughout his report the archaeologist supplies parallels from both similar and dissimilar cultures. Everything is written to help the reader whether he is a professional or a member of the public. Usually a bibliography goes at the end of the article, as do special topics such as the museums where the finds are kept and the list of acknowledgments of help. Modern archaeology reports contain appendices by such specialists as botanists, zoologists, geologists, metallurgists, textile experts etc. They should be skilfully cross-linked with the main text.

There are many other ways of collecting and disseminating archaeological facts: card index systems describing finds or sites, kept not by individuals but in museums or universities or the headquarters of societies, are invaluable. Another useful thing is a system of promptly published short abstracts on all archaeological articles produced in one country enabling an archaeologist to get a bird's eye view of the work.

Information retrieval techniques are essential for archaeological research.

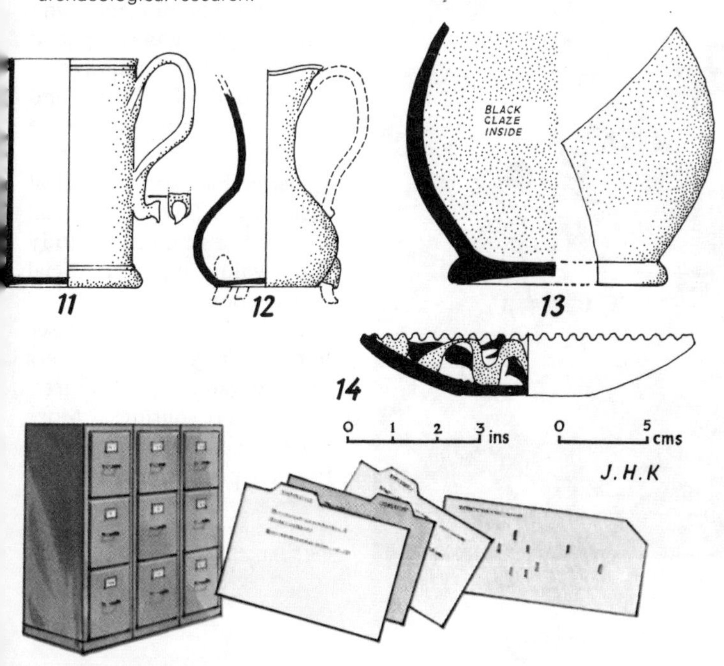

Archaeological Societies

With the growth of archaeology in many countries the amateur can increase his chances of becoming an effective part-time worker. He has, of course, to persuade professionals and archaeological officialdom that he is neither a crank nor a dilettante. Despite increased state control which is intended to check both philistinism and treasure hunters, the amateur has made himself increasingly useful and furthered archaeological enquiry.

The volunteer has to impress by his diligence and initiative in *observing* and *recording*. This requires a background of reading and museum visits that has to be enhanced by membership of a reputable archaeological society. A well-run local society is a stimulus to study and a valuable aid to official archaeology.

First, a society should see to the *training* of its members by organizing lectures, classes and outings. More experienced members and friendly professionals should

Good training and field work is the strength of a society.

do all they can to raise standards, thus benefitting archaeology as a whole.

Practical work is important but there should not be a childish haste to excavate. Many other useful activities besides digging come under the banner of archaeology: clearing vegatation from ancient sites, restoring old walls or archaic industrial plant and plotting or photographing antiquities and old buildings.

The archaeological 'health' of a country is to be measured by the efficiency and standards of local societies. A handful of renowned and brilliant specialists in high places is not enough.

The running of a society can be reduced to a formalized structure. But officers have to be good sociologists and psychologists. Extraordinary things go on: scapegoats occur, small groups hog activities and we have what is politely called the 'clash of personalities'. Such unpleasant facts are, unfortunately, as much a part of archaeology as the rain that stops a dig or a collapse of soil on diggers.

Sometimes the amateur should leave it to the professionals.

The Museum

Fortunately few people nowadays see museums as dreary or dusty places. But many do not realize that a good museum should be like the proverbial iceberg: most of the mass below the surface. If everything is on show, the visitor tires in eye and spirit. Thus a good museum might display only 1% of its collections. Exhibits will be chosen for their beauty, or as local types or as dating specimens. Displays should be changed at not too long intervals.

A museum has to be a depository for much material that would be lost or unrecognized in private hands. But scholars and the serious amateur will want access to the reference collections of a museum. So special cases, stores or galleries are needed. Often the real reputation of a museum hinges on the efficiency of its backroom stores and catalogues.

A museum must not be a warehouse of unwanted things. It should be the home of systematically collected samples of man's culture. A museum is not just for scholars, all society can benefit from it. For example, a textile designer can find ancient motifs for modern patterns; a film director can get authentic background for a period film; a young production engineer sees how basic techniques and basic prejudices can guide or hinder progress. Most important of all the child learns in the museums to love history as a subject.

In the past people regarded a museum as a storage box into which one might respectfully peep. Today a curator can visualize his museum as a lens – or, if you like, a television screen – in which the past becomes not merely vivid but relevant. From seeing change in the past we are made to focus on change in the present and the future.

Well-run regional museums do not depend so much on eminent curators as on an enthusiastic staff. Without a conservation officer and a staff of archaeological explorers and folk life specialists a museum becomes a sluggish tortoise. These in turn depend on technicians, photographers, display artists, carpenters, painters, cleaners, security men, sales staff (visitors like to buy postcards, booklets and replicas) and many others. Up-to-date museums have a large staff of specialists who concentrate their attention on dealing with the interests of schools and children.

A good museum has complex stores and services and simple displays

Kinds of archaeology

People who make archaeology the great interest of their lives can be too specialized in their tastes. Interest in Egyptology, or the Romans or the Maya, swamps and paralyzes curiosity about other periods and people. While it is wise to concentrate on certain topics, it is foolish to do so to the extent that one is incapable of being interested about other aspects of archaeology. There are not enough archaeologists and there are too many regions needing all-rounders for sorting out a policy of research and exploration.

Prehistory deals with the story of man or of peoples that lived before they possessed writings and records. Prehistoric peoples left no writings and inscriptions: all we can learn about them is by the detective methods of the archaeologist. Occasionally prehistoric peoples who had no writing are mentioned by the Greeks or Romans or the Egyptians. One

An Australian limekiln. Medieval mason marks. Inca wall

Restored 15th-cent. house, Wales Viking brooches
Dress and ornament can also be archaeology

can have a battle, for example, between the historical Marius or Caesar and a 'prehistoric' Celtic people, but the general idea of prehistory is clear.

Some prehistorians may enjoy a spell working on the archaeology of historical peoples. There is a satisfaction in linking a Chinese bronze to a particular dynasty or in finding an account book recording the building of a castle wall in Wales in the reign of Edward I. A few decades ago many people thought archaeology 'ended' with the Romans, but nowadays medieval archaeology has greatly helped economic and art historians. There has also arisen a greater concern for industrial archaeology: this is not merely the study of the material remains of the Industrial Revolution, for it can be systematic research into development of trades, technology and production of all ages and lands.

A good archaeologist will try to spread his interests widely to get the stimuli that always come when one meets people working in adjoining fields of study.

A SELF-TESTING QUIZ

Some of the objects below can be identified from pictures earlier in the book. A few items are of a new type; they are introduced to help you think about unknown objects. The answers are printed upside down on p. 155.

Answers

1. Skull of *Homo sapiens neanderthalensis,* France
2. Carved figure from late Mesolithic village in Yugoslavia
3. Plastered skull from pre-pottery Neolithic, Jericho
4. Neolithic pot, China
5. Neolithic pot, Wiltshire
6. Greek amphora, Athens, 86 B.C.
7. Flint dagger of Beaker period, found in the Thames at Battersea
8. Beaker, late Neolithic, from Oxfordshire
9. Clovis point from America, c. 9000 B.C.
10. Folsom point from America, c. 8000 B.C.
11. Mousterian scraper, France
12. Geometric Mesolithic flints, France
13. Handaxe, France, Palaeolithic
14. Knight, 12th century, on tapestry, Norway
15. Roman milestone from Leicestershire A.D. 120–121
16. Engraved pebble, Upper Palaeolithic, France : a hairy mammoth
17. Norse-type sword found in U.S.S.R., 11th century A.D.
18. Bronze Age rapier, Devon, c. 1000 B.C.

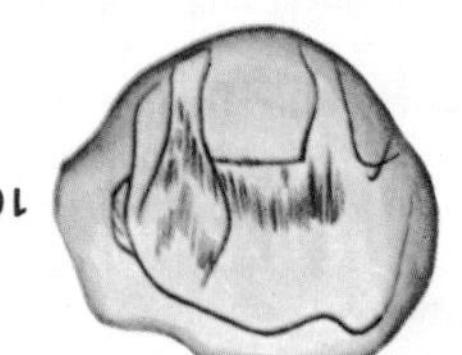

16

14

15

17

18

FURTHER READING AND STUDY

Bacon, Edward (ed.) *Vanished Civilizations*. Thames and Hudson, London. *1963*

Bordes, F. *The Old Stone Age*. Weidenfeld and Nicolson, London. *1968*

Burland, Cottie. *The People of the Ancient Americas*. Paul Hamlyn, Feltham. *1970*

Ceram, C. W. *A Picture History of Archaeology*. Thames and Hudson, London. *1958*

Childe, V. G. *The Prehistory of European Society*. Penguin, Harmondsworth. *1958*

Clark, J. D. E. *The Prehistory of Africa*. Thames and Hudson, London. *1970*

Clark, J. G. D. *World Prehistory*. Cambridge University Press. *1969*

Cole, J. M. and Higgs, E. S. *The Archaeology of Early Man*. Faber and Faber, London. *1969*

Cookson, M. B. *Photography for Archaeologists*. Parrish, London. *1954*

Day, Michael H. *Fossil Man*. Hamlyn, Feltham. *1969*

Desroches-Noblecourt, C. *Tutankhamun*. Penguin Books, Harmondsworth *1965*

Edoux, Henri-Paul. *In Search of Lost Worlds*. The Hamlyn Group, Feltham. *1970*

Hudson, Kenneth. *Industrial Archaeology*. Methuen, *1966*

Kenyon, K. *Beginning in Archaeology*. J. M. Dent and Sons Ltd, London. *1964*

Piggott, Stuart (ed.). *The Dawn of Civilization*. Thames and Hudson, London. *1967*

Wheeler, Sir Mortimer. *Archaeology from the Earth*. Penguin Books, Harmondsworth. *1956*

Wood, Eric S. *Collin's Field Guide to Archaeology*. Collins, London. *1968*

Museums

Listed below are a few of the more important world collections: the British Museum, London; the National History Museum, London; the Australian Museum, Sydney; Macleay Museum of Natural History, Sydney; American Museum of Natural History, New York; Chicago Natural History Museum, United States; United States National Museum, Washington D.C.; Musée des Antiquités Nationales, Paris; Musée de L'Homme, Paris; Museo Nazionale Romano, Rome; Museum für Volkerkunde, Berlin; Museum für Volkerkunde, Vienna.

INDEX

Page numbers in bold type refer to illustrations

SOME OTHER TITLES IN THIS SERIES

Natural History

The Animal Kingdom
Animals of Australia & New Zealand
Animals of South America
Animals of Southern Asia
Bird Behaviour
Birds of Prey
Butterflies
Evolution of Life
Fishes of the World
Fossil Man
A Guide to the Seashore

Gardening

Chrysanthemums
Garden Flowers

Popular Science

Astronomy
Atomic Energy
Computers at Work
The Earth
Electricity
Electronics

Arts

Architecture
Clocks and Watches
Glass
Jewellery

General Information

Arms and Armour
Coins and Medals
Flags
Guns
Military Uniforms
Rockets and Missiles

Domestic Animals & Pets

Budgerigars
Cats
Dog Care
Dogs

Domestic Science

Flower Arranging

History & Mythology

Discovery of
- Africa
- Australia
- Japan

Discovery of
- North America
- South America
- The American West